*Nature
Lover's
Guide
to the
Big
Thicket*

NUMBER
FIFTEEN:

The W. L.
Moody, Jr.,
Natural
History
Series

Nature Lover's Guide to the Big Thicket

Howard Peacock

Foreword by Maxine Johnston

Texas A&M University Press

The paper used in this book meets the minimum
requirements of the American National Standard for
Permanence of Paper for Printed Library Materials,
Z39.48-1984. Binding materials have been chosen for
durability.

Library of Congress Cataloging-in-Publication Data

Peacock, Howard H., 1925–
    Nature lover's guide to the Big Thicket / by
Howard Peacock ;
foreword by Maxine Johnston.
        p.   cm. — (The W. L. Moody, Jr., natural his-
tory series ; no. 15)
    Includes bibliographical references (p.   ) and
index.
    ISBN 0-89096-589-7 (cloth). — ISBN 0-89096-596-X
(paper)
    1. Natural history—Texas—Big Thicket National
Preserve. 2. Natural history—Texas—Big Thicket
National Preserve—Guidebooks. 3. Big Thicket National Preserve (Tex.)—Guidebooks. I. Title.
II. Series.
QH105.T4P43   1994
574.9764—dc20   93-38508
                                               CIP

To neighbors and strangers
who like to walk woods and fields,
and who grow to love such places
as the Big Thicket.

And to the plants and animals whose species
Once lived in the Big Thicket
But now are gone forever, "exterminated" as they say,
"Extinct," disappeared from the planet,
Just gone.
The earth would have to begin all over again
And do the same things over billions of years, exactly,
For you extinct ones to be reborn,
And in your singular integrity to
Flourish.

Contents

Contents

Illustrations

Photographs by the author except as noted in captions.

Foreword

Visitors and big-city neighbors have needed a hip-pocket guidebook to the Big Thicket for a long time. For fifty years, the curious came, asked local folks where it was, and were told it was over there near Saratoga—or if they were in Saratoga, it might be over there near Warren, or, better still, the Jack Gore Baygall. What to see—and where—was another problem because all the land was privately owned and a person trespassed at risk.

The lucky visitors found Lance Rosier, "Mr. Big Thicket," who served as an interpreter of the Big Woods from his youth until his death in 1970. Lance's character and philosophy contributed as no other's could to the quality sometimes called the "mystique of the Big Thicket." He shared his matchless knowledge and stories of the Thicket with all comers—scientists, students, writers, public officials, members of civic clubs of all kinds.

Other visitors may have found John Knight of Segno, or quiet, perceptive Harold Nicholas of Saratoga, or the colorful, flamboyant Neal Wright, and have fallen in love with the Thicket from their widely differing approaches. Perhaps the most knowledgeable, determined, and influential of all the Thicket guides after Lance was Geraldine Watson of Silsbee, who introduced junketing members of the U.S. Congress, inquisitive biologists, and a legion of conservationists to her structured Big Thicket.

Then there was fire-eating Archer Fullingim. As editor of the *Kountze News* in its heydey, he trumpeted the glory of his personal "Holy Ghost Thicket" over the years, not only in his newspaper but also as a featured guest on many national and regional talk shows. At the same time, Professor Claude McLeod devoted his brilliant scientific rationale to provide and publish a territorial definition of the Big Thicket. Somehow, those two disparate souls seemed cut from a kindred mold.

The pioneer interpreters in different ways all helped pave the way for the establishment, in 1974, of the Big Thicket National Preserve. That was the signal for the National Park Service to arrive on the scene and begin administering and protecting 84,550 acres of most of the significant Thicket ecosystems. And now, finally, visitors can go Thicket-stompin' without fear of trespass.

It's my observation that the Thicket communicates best with solitary wanderers, but it also speaks to companionable spirits. An important trick on the trail is to shift one's focus from the big scene to the minuscule. Take your time, folks. The Big Thicket is not a hurry-place.

Howard Peacock has special qualities needed for a Big Thicket interpreter. He's been poking around these woods since he was a boy in Beaumont. As a free-lance journalist and author, he has written articles about Thicket facts and lore for many regional and national publications—*Texas Highways* magazine, *The World and I,* the pre-Valdez *Exxon USA,* major daily newspapers, and *Fodor's Guides,* to name a few. He introduced young readers, and older ones, too, to the Thicket's beauty, diversity, and history in his book, *The Big Thicket of Texas: America's Ecological Wonder,* and in the 1991 keepsake book, *The Nature of Texas.*

In the 1960s and 1970s Howard was a leader in the Save the Big Thicket national campaign, earning the nickname "Tush Hog," usually hung on the meanest old rooter in the woods. He served as president of the Big Thicket Association in 1975–76 and chaired the Arid Sandylands Committee that worked with Arthur Temple of Temple-Eastex, the corporate landowners (now Temple-Inland), to establish the Roy E. Larsen Sandyland Sanctuary. He has conducted museum seminars on the Big Thicket, workshops for nature writers, and has spoken eloquently for the Thicket on such TV programs as "Texas Country Roads," "Ray Miller's Texas," and the national PBS hit "Wildflowers," hosted by Helen Hayes.

In backyard gatherings, controversial public hearings, and best of all, explorations of our woods and meadows,

I've shared quality time with the Tush Hog. In these settings I've become keenly aware of his strong character and absolute integrity. He's a friend, a defender of the environmental faith, and your Big Thicket guide par excellence.

—Maxine Johnston

Foreword

Acknowledgments

I'm warmly grateful—

To the Beaumont Hilton Hotel, its general manager and sales director, for real hospitality during the field work for this *Guide.*

To Jack Zilker, founder and head of NPL Laboratories in Houston and a thoughtful conservationist, who provided valuable photo-processing services.

To the staff of the National Park Service of the Big Thicket National Preserve—superintendent Ron Switzer, David Baker, Doug Bradley, Col. Mike Livingston, Bob Valen, and a passel of rangers.

To *Texas Highways* magazine editors Jack Lowry, Rosemary Williams, Laura Black, and Jill Bates, who supported my efforts as a writer and tolerated my eccentricities as a grouch.

To John Reed, concerned parent and citizen, excellent pharmacist, boss of J&S Drugs of Woodville, who provided help with his magic copying machine.

Talk about support—in various ways and at odd times (and hell, ain't most times odd) these friends gave it: Pat and Eleanor Blair, Bud and Marge Payne, Dayton and Jean Pickett, Mary Jean Shofner, Ruth Sublett, Jan and Willie Wilson, Ginny Fife, famed novelist Janece Hudson, Charlie Dillingham, Curtis Garner, Jackson Porter, Ken Bryan, Ann Roberts, Betty Warren, Helen Roe, Iris Ballew, Jimmy and Barbara Rowe, Roy and Linda Rollins, Gus and Beth Galiano, Zenobia Brake, Allen and Bobbie Commander, Dee McFarland, Lynn Lowrey, Larry Phillips, Ginny Martin, Carla Stewart, Jerry and Katherine Mize, Kelly Strenge, John and Doris Neibel, Laine Potter, Rochelle Gassiott, Harold Phenix, Howard Rosser, Kevin and Ann Wagner, Otis Thomas, Gary Hennigan, Sharon Steen, Peyton Walters, Warren and Ann Kocher, Annette Merton, Lily Rose Claiborne, the Rescue Squad of Roane

County, Tennessee, and members of the Third Thursday Gang of Tyler County.

Two fishermen of note in Big Thicket streams, Harold Ogden and Dave Bordelon, shared their knowledge and honest-to-God truthful experiences.

Acknowl-edgments   Missy Ogden of Colmesneil typed much of the manuscript.

One of the best things about writing this book was meeting and working with Camille North, my editor at Texas A&M University Press. Patient, good-humored, professional to a high degree, she forgave my many transgressions of authordom and turned me firmly to the needs at hand. This small tribute, and a Cajun fig-pecan pie I made for her, are poor recompense.

Claude McLeod, a great biologist and teacher at Sam Houston State University for many years, a creative and careful expert in the field and at his desk, and a warmhearted friend, furnished inspiration for this *Guide,* simply by his presence and the sound of his strong, kindly voice.

—Howard Peacock

*Nature
Lover's
Guide
to the
Big
Thicket*

Introducing America's Ark 1

Welcome to one of the world's special places.

The Big Thicket of Southeast Texas is America's first sanctuary of nature to be declared a national preserve. It's also among a few places in the entire earth to be chosen by scientists of the United Nations for its Man and the Biosphere project.

That project aims "to conserve the genetic resources of the earth's plants and animals, to foster research, and to monitor changes now taking place in the earth's natural systems."

Whoa! Those are heady words for a little corner pocket of Southeast Texas.

What makes the Big Thicket a world-class place is its spectacular diversity of plant and animal life. Lance Rosier, the late "Saint Francis of the Big Thicket," as he was titled by a justice of the Supreme Court who followed Lance into the forest, once estimated that the Thicket harbored at least one thousand species of flowering plants.

Of birds, today's count ranges from about two hundred species to twice that many and more, depending on the numbers of subspecies and migrants one counts. Reptiles: about fifty kinds, from the blue-tailed skink and yellow-bellied king snake to the Mississippi alligator. Mammals: between twenty and twenty-five species, from mink to bobcat to white-tailed deer. Wild orchids: more than thirty kinds. Mushrooms, liverworts, algae, and their ilk: yet untotaled. Insects: just say the Big Thicket is an entomologist's paradise. Wild trees and shrubs: about two hundred species, including champions discovered and yet to be discovered. Carnivorous (meat-eating) plants: four of the five kinds found in all of North America. And so on.

Big Thicket National Preserve and *Big Thicket region* are two expressions used in this *Guide* and in other writings. What's the difference?

The Big Thicket National Preserve is a collection of

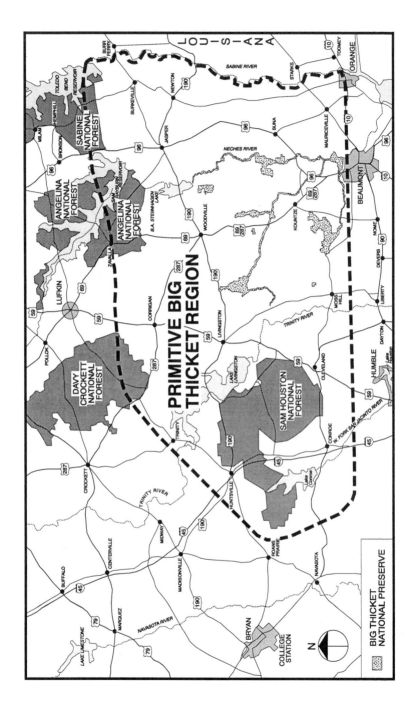

fifteen units in fragments of land and water corridors, designated by the U.S. Congress as federal property bought and protected for the education and enjoyment of the American people, and administered by the National Park Service. At this writing, the number of acres under federal protection totals 95,316.

The Big Thicket region refers to the entire area of about 3,500,000 acres in Southeast Texas known as the "primitive Big Thicket," before communities, industries, oil and lumber booms, real estate developments, and other spoor of civilization carved chunks out of the woods, except for a few inaccessible spots. The Big Thicket region reaches from Pine Island Bayou on the south to the Sabine River on the east, north for about sixty or so miles, westward along a geological line that passes below Lufkin to about Shiro or Roan's Prairie, then swings southward in a modified curve to the mixed-grass prairies of east Liberty County, and on to Pine Island Bayou.

Recently, scientists revised earlier counts of different ecosystems found in the Big Thicket National Preserve, upgrading the number from eight to ten. They range from arid sandylands to cypress sloughs, from lordly upland forests to mud-crusted flats dappled by palmetto fronds. Few if any places of comparable size on earth can lay claim to so many unique clusters, to such richness of natural variety. Little wonder, then, that the Big Thicket has been called the "Biological Crossroads of North America" and "America's Ark."

The ten ecosystems in the Big Thicket National Preserve do not include another distinct biological society, Mixed-Grass Prairie, which is usually associated with the great central plains, or heartland America. An example of that community is found outside the Preserve, but well within the Big Thicket region, between Batson and Moss Hill in Hardin County.

What all the uppity scientific jargon comes down to mean to the American family on an outing, or to retired folks refreshing their youthful sense of curiosity, or to a jangled business employee seeking a spot of serenity and refuge from urban thrash, is that the Big Thicket offers a matchless place to enjoy nature anew, in endless relationships of plants and creatures.

Don't plan to hike the Big Thicket. A hiker expects to cover distance. Plan to stroll the Thicket—or saunter, to use Thoreau's word, pausing often to let your eyes squint and your ears pick up rustlings and callings. Nature here often speaks in stutters or soft slurs. Expect to lean on trees and sit on stumps. Your mind is apt to meander, like that butterfly catching the breeze, or that bejewelled beetle searching last night's leaf litter, or a nearby creeklet puddling around a tangle of roots before easing on south.

The spectacular diversity of the Big Thicket began in the region of the current state of Wisconsin. Glaciers formed there in the last Ice Age and sucked up waters of the Atlantic Ocean, in turn causing waters of the Gulf of Mexico to recede, exposing the soil of Southeast Texas. Then the opposite happened. As the glaciers warmed and melted, the oceans rose, flooding the land and depositing new silt and debris over the old. Then came another freeze and suck-up, followed by another melting and flooding. This process happened at least four times, according to geologists, beginning some two to three million years ago and ending about ten thousand years ago. A lot of seeds, roots, and silts were deposited in these back-and-forth washings. Rivers and streams from all directions added their fertile contributions to those of the Gulf. In such a manner were the soils of the Big Thicket composed and shaped into low hills, valleys, flatlands. One authority estimates the Thicket contains more than fifty kinds of soil. A diversity of soils is a primary reason for the vast variety of plant life and, by "domino effect," animal life as well.

In the old days, the Thicket served as a haven for such storied creatures as mammoths, mastodons, capybara, and tapir. About seven thousand years ago, wanderers from Asia, already having crossed the Bering Straits and continuing south, passed through the Thicket, leaving telltale stone implements to mark their stay. These mysterious migrants may have been the ancestors of later Indian tribes with familiar names.

"Big Woods," the Indians called the region of the Thicket.

Four tribes—Bidai, Deadose, Patiri, and Akiosa—dwelt in various parts of the area, all speaking the Atakapan language. The Bidais also spoke a tongue learned from their highly accomplished neighbors living just north of the Thicket, the Caddoes.

In the eighteenth century, two tribes from southeastern America, the Alabamas and Coushattas, traveled into the Thicket and made settlements among the trees. Today, their descendants own a 4,181-acre reservation between Woodville and Livingston and there operate one of the major tourist attractions in Texas.

Spanish explorers penetrated the Thicket in the late seventeenth century. Today, a long-abandoned site on private land in Tyler County, fronting on a stretch of Neches River, has a marker, Fort Teran, named after the first governor of the province of the Tejas, Domingo de los Ríos Terán. A cache of Spanish gold, of course, lies buried somewhere near the site, or perhaps over or under the river. So goes the legend.

American pioneers first rode into the Thicket in the 1820s; another wave came in the 1830s. Folklore, quite believable, says that they changed the region's name from the "Big Woods" of the Indians to "Big Thicket," a cussing tribute to the impassable groves of titi (*Cyrilla racemiflora*) that blocked their paths. *Titi*, an Indian word, became "tight-eye" in the vernacular. A body still can't ride, walk, or crawl ten feet into a titi thicket without narrowing his or her eyes against walls of splintery branches.

Settlers' cabins and crops soon pocked the pristine forests that had covered the Indians' Big Woods. Vast logging operations began in the post–Civil War years and eventually removed all but slivers of virgin timber. Around the turn of the century, wild oil booms at Sour Lake, Saratoga, and Batson spurred drilling for black gold; scattered drilling under strict environmental regulations continues to the present hour. Today, wilderness areas in the Thicket total less than an estimated 300,000 acres. Scarcely a few of those acres can claim to be pristine, like the wilderness of the Indians that covered more than three million acres.

"Save the Big Thicket!" became the rallying cry of conservationists as early as the 1920s. A fifty-year fight by grass-roots citizens and scientists to set aside representative remnants of America's Ark resulted in the establishment of the Big Thicket National Preserve. The historic legislation passed by Congress and signed by President Gerald Ford on October 11, 1974, specified 84,550 acres divided into twelve units. On a map, the units resemble a freewheeling version of the Rorschach blotches, sometimes more than fifty miles apart. But each contains one or more types of the ten major ecosystems of the Big Thicket region.

On July 1, 1993, President Bill Clinton signed legislation adding 10,766 acres in three units to the National Preserve. Two of the new units protect the vital water corridors flowing through the heart of the Thicket, from the southern edge of the Big Sandy Unit to the Neches River outflow above Beaumont. The new northern segment, named the Big Sandy Corridor Unit, comprises 4,497 acres. The new southern segment, named the Village Creek Corridor Unit, adds 4,793 acres. Also, 1,476 acres of biologically valuable and picturesque land on the Neches River, due east of the Beech Creek Unit, have been preserved and named the Canyonlands Unit. Again, the prime mover in Congress behind these additions was U.S. Representative Charlie Wilson of Lufkin, who carried the original legislation for the Big Thicket National Preserve to success. The additions bring the total number of acres in the Preserve to 95,316. The 1993 bill specifies that the new 10,766 acres are to be acquired by exchanges of national forest land with timber companies that own the tracts designated for the three added units.

Chapter 3 of this *Guide* introduces each unit, shows you how to get there and suggests what to look for. Be mindful of the season of your visit. Many flowers and creatures are particular about timing. Nothing in the Thicket occupies center stage all the time, except stray alligators. The scene constantly changes. A given trail looks one way today, subtly different next week.

In that chapter, too, you'll find the specific ecosystems evolving within each unit of the National Preserve and how to recognize them. In the field, you may discover a transition zone—the line of demarcation between one ecosystem and a totally different one.

Spend a few minutes with your *Guide* just to get acquainted with facts, images, and Big Thicket lore. Dog-ear the pages you want to come back to, unless you have a librarian's horror of such a practice. After all, this book is your trail companion. If used properly, it will get bent up, streaked with mosquito squashings, stained with creek water.

The best place to start a visit to the Thicket is the log-cabin Information Center on FM 420, which intersects U.S. 69 about eight miles north of Kountze. Turn east on FM 420 and go 2.5 miles to the Information Center. (Sometime in the latter 1990s, if all goes well, a permanent, multipurpose Visitors Center will be built near the U.S. 69–FM 420 intersection. Then, that will be the place to start.)

Check in at the Information Center, then start sauntering, as Thoreau says, down the winding, forty-five–minute trail to the cathedral of giant cypresses. Sit for a while and gaze at those trees, buttressed on the floodplain of Village Creek. If you set the monkey mind at rest, and just see and hear and feel for a while, you'll understand why some people keep returning to the Big Thicket and its unrivaled variety of ecosystems, year after year.

2 The Ecosystems

In one word, here lies the secret to the Big Thicket's claim to a world-class distinction. The Thicket contains more kinds of ecosystems than any other place of similar size in North America, perhaps in the world.

What's an *ecosystem?* Like most human enterprises, science has developed its own jargon. But don't let the word throw you. It's simply a place where certain plants, animals, soils and minerals, bacteria, fungi, and algae form a community and function as a unit in nature. *Eco* refers to home or community, *system* to function.

Other organisms stay away because they don't like the weather, the kinds of food and drink available, the resident creatures, or for other reasons. Polar bears don't like the desert and pitcher-plants don't grow atop the tundra.

Borders of these natural communities are not inviolate, however. Invaders of the plant and animal kingdoms constantly try to penetrate other ecosystems. That's probably why some plants release chemicals from their roots to poison other plants encroaching on their territory, a tactic known as the allelopathic effect. Black walnut trees, for example, do an especially good job of root-zapping plants that get too close.

You'll see terms in nature books and articles that mean just about the same thing as ecosystems: terms like *plant communities, plant associations, vegetation types.* This *Guide* uses ecosystems because it includes the whole natural neighborhood of living and inanimate beings.

At least ten, maybe more, ecosystems dovetail in the Big Thicket. The National Park Service identifies them as follows:

Baygall	Palmetto-Hardwood Flats
Beech-Magnolia-Loblolly	Pine Savannah Wetlands
Cypress Slough	River Edge
Longleaf Pine Upland	Roadside
Oak-Gum Floodplain	Arid Sandylands

Another ecosystem is pointed out by naturalists Geraldine Watson and Geyata Ajilvsgi, but it is not represented in the Big Thicket National Preserve: Mixed-Grass Prairie.

A word here about Watson and Ajilvsgi. They'll be quoted often in this chapter and elsewhere in this *Guide.* Watson grew up in the Thicket and has observed and recorded its wonders for a lifetime. She's the author of an excellent booklet, *Big Thicket Plant Ecology: An Introduction,* and a forthcoming book about the Neches River. Ajilvsgi, an accomplished photographer and scientifically trained naturalist, has produced two invaluable reference works, *Wild Flowers of the Big Thicket,* and *The Wildflowers of Texas.* Her name reveals her Cherokee Indian heritage.

In addition, two distinguished ecological botanists, Dr. Paul Harcombe of Rice University and Dr. Peter Marks of Cornell University, are quoted. They co-authored a bedrock scientific survey, *Forest Vegetation of the Big Thicket, Southeast Texas,* an eighteen-page monograph published in 1981 by the Ecological Society of America.

To the rest of us, it's confusing for authorities such as those above, and the experts on the staff of the National Park Service, to use different names for the various ecosystems. Sometimes the names are considerably different, sometimes not much. What Watson and the National Park Service call "Arid Sandylands," Ajilvsgi calls "Oak-Farkleberry Sandylands" and Harcombe-Marks split into three other designations. One sunny day all authorities on ecosystems should meet on a sandbar and decide on simple, descriptive terms that everybody can use forever after.

"Simplify! Clarify! Simplify! Clarify!" urged one of the greatest naturalists of all, Henry David Thoreau.

This *Guide* will stick to the ecosystem names that the National Park Service uses. After all, most visitors to the Big Thicket will get their bearings from the National Park Service, either at the new Visitors Center on FM 420 or at one of the National Park Service (NPS) ranger stations.

Wherever you explore, bear in mind that there's no such thing as a perfectly composed ecosystem. For example, a Cypress Slough will have elements that don't show up on the official tally; so will any ecosystem. You'll see loblolly pines and sweetgums and wax-myrtles just about everywhere in the Big Thicket. In some instances, they play very important roles; in others, they just happen to be around.

Can you spot the following trees: southern magnolia, longleaf pine, loblolly pine, bald cypress? How about these: American beech, swamp tupelo, shortleaf pine, sweet-bay magnolia, white oak? If you checked some of these, you're well on your way to recognizing ecosystems. Those trees are among the so-called dominants of the different ecosystems.

Another buzz word—*dominants.* It simply means any of one or more kinds of organism (like a species of tree or shrub) in an ecological community that exerts a controlling influence on the organisms present. That's straight from *Webster's Ninth New Collegiate Dictionary,* an excellent definer for nature lovers to keep by the armchair.

Strong recommendation: take a field trip or two with a knowledgeable guide who will point out differences between ecosystems to you and your group. Such guides can be found in nearby nature clubs and environmental organizations.

And another recommendation for studious Big Thicket nature lovers. Obtain copies of the excellent checklists published by the staff of the National Preserve Headquarters. They're not complete and probably can't be, but they're terrific for field trip records. A fairly new checklist, for example, names about 450 species of flowering plants with a date of record for the blooming of each species.

Now, off to the woods and fields.

Baygall

When many people think of the Big Thicket, they get an image of dense vine-tangled woods shimmering in shallow water, a shadowy place except for shafts of sunlight filtering through a canopy of broad-trunked trees. Large ferns and chartreuse-colored mats of sphagnum moss form abstract patterns in the gloom. That's an image of a baygall.

Typical tangle of the Baygall ecosystem. Jack Gore Baygall Unit.

It's the storied setting of the Traditional Bear-Hunter's Thicket that surrounds Saratoga, but it also appears in other parts of the Big Thicket. Jack Gore Baygall, brooding on the western shore of the Neches River bottom, is considered the largest baygall in the world, covering approximately twelve square miles.

Characteristics of this ecosystem include very high acidity (pH 4.5 is common for soils and water here), very poor drainage, and a perpetual bogginess afoot. Of special interest are hanging bogs, which occur on some slopes, and succession ponds, in which large depressions in clayey land have filled with water and are gradually changing into forest land. This intriguing transition results from a succession of plants—first grasses, then shrubs, then trees— dying in the standing water, their increasing debris decomposing to form different soil materials, thus inviting other plants to take hold.

Scientists detect differences between acid bogs and baygalls, but the current National Park Service listings group these acid-loving environments together.

The word *baygall* derives from two trees found in profuse clusters in these places—sweet-bay magnolia and gallberry holly. Other large trees found here are swamp tupelo and bald cypress. Common shrubs in baygalls are waxmyrtle, titi, red bay, and Virginia sweetspire.

At the proper seasons, you might come across these wildflowers in bloom: Texas trillium, fragrant water lily, sweet pepperbush, white azalea, floating heart, Joe-Pyeweed, water-spider orchid and rose pogonia orchid, and the carnivorous bladderwort.

Baygalls are found in the following units of the Big Thicket National Preserve:

Beech Creek Unit	Hickory Creek Savannah Unit
Lance Rosier Unit	Jack Gore Baygall–Neches
Big Sandy Creek Unit	Bottom Units
Turkey Creek Unit	

Arid Sandylands

More college biology classes take field trips into the Arid Sandylands than to any other single ecosystem in the Big Thicket. Indeed, it might be the most tantalizing living laboratory of all the Thicket's environments. "It's the least expected plant association found in the Big Thicket," says naturalist Geyata Ajilvsgi.

What are desert plants—prickly pear cactus and yucca—doing in the woods of rain-drenched Southeast Texas? One reason is that they thrive in sand. And great piles of sand have been dumped here over the ages by Big Thicket streams. Unlike typical deserts, these tracts receive almost fifty inches of rain in an average year. But the sand is so porous that the water percolates right through it, leaving the surface and upper layers of the soil ready to be dried by the next hot sun. To protect themselves from this drying effect, some plants have developed waxy coatings, hairs, deep root systems, and small leaf surfaces to help them retain moisture.

You will find examples of Arid Sandylands in five units of the Big Thicket National Preserve, but the best place to explore this ecosystem is the Roy E. Larsen Sandyland Sanctuary, located a few miles west of Silsbee. (See Chapter 9.) It's owned and managed by the Texas Nature Conservancy and is open to the public daily. The Larsen Sanctuary sits on high terraces of Village Creek and reveals a peculiar mixture of drylands and wetlands, interspersed with woodlands. "A biology class can look at more plant associations here in one day than elsewhere in several days," commented one teacher.

Not the least remarkable feature of this ecosystem is that it provides habitat for more species of wildflowers than any other environment in the Big Thicket, except the pine wetlands, according to naturalist Geraldine Watson. She estimates more than 340 species of wildflowers flourish in the Arid Sandylands.

Here, baygalls and hardwood forests exist side-by-side with sun-parched sand dunes. One small baygall broods only a few hundred yards from the trailhead. The visitor

Yucca, sand, and scrub brush in the Arid Sandylands.

treks through sand along a high bluff overlooking Village Creek. To one side of the path, a dense stand of hardwoods rises on a ridge sloping down to a cypress slough; on the other side, scrub oak, cactus and patches of sun-baked sand lead to the dank, dark baygall awaiting ahead.

Alligator Grass Pond, one of the most popular sites for naturalists and hikers, is located in the Sanctuary about a half-mile east of Village Creek, north of a railroad track that splits the area on a diagonal northwest-southeast line. Alligators took up residence near the middle of the pond, clearing out the aquatic plants and digging out the bottom to help them survive summer droughts. Rare species of plants have been spotted on islands floating in the pond.

A short walk away, the Triple Ponds depict three phases of wetlands evolution. South Pond is relatively more open and deeper than the other two. Middle Pond is filled with sedges, and North Pond holds a heavy growth of trees that tolerate wet feet.

Sweetspire Baygall is another popular site for biology classes and nature lovers. Stretching about four miles in length, east of Triple Ponds, it lies in the middle of the original sandyland formation halfway between Village Creek on the west and an ancient bluff line on the east that now harbors Beech-Magnolia-Loblolly woodlands. Sweetspire Baygall is home to notably large specimens of titi, wax-myrtle, and gallberry holly, and once contained the national champion gallberry holly.

Ecologists Harcombe and Marks divide the Arid Sandy-lands complex into three environments. One they call Sand-hill Pine Forests—"an open woodland with low tree and shrub densities, a relatively sparse herb layer, and much exposed sand." In this setting, bluejack oak and post oak are dominant trees, with longleaf, loblolly, and shortleaf pines also in the overstory. Abundant small trees include yaupon and dogwood.

Another they call the Upper Slope Pine-Oak Forest, described as "a closed-canopy forest with a moderately well-developed shrub layer." Here the shortleaf pine dominates with southern red oak, longleaf and loblolly pines, and blackjack oak as co-dominants. Associates include post oak, sweetgum, and white oak. Besides yaupon and dogwood in the understory, you find American beauty-berry and sassafras.

They also delineate a Mid-Slope Oak Pine Forest, "generally taller with a more closed canopy and a greater proportion of hardwoods in the overstory . . ." The overstory dominants include white oak, southern red oak, and loblolly and shortleaf pine. Next to them: sweetgum, black gum, and red maple. And, in the understory, dogwood, yaupon, and American holly.

Naturalist Watson believes the dominant trees in the sandhills along Village Creek are longleaf pine and bluejack oak, with farkleberry abundant as the understory shrub. The drier northern sandhills, she notes, grade into populations of blackjack, post oak, and black hickory.

A slightly different tack is reported by naturalist Ajilvsgi. She calls the ecosystem "Oak-Farkleberry Sandylands" but agrees with Watson on the dominants.

It takes a seasoned eye and a score-keeping mind to recognize these distinctions. Moreover, changes occur yearly as Village Creek continues to shift vast quantities of sand in its windings. Every flood rearranges the banks.

Wildflowers brighten these sand fields in the spring, summer and into autumn. Among them are Louisiana yucca, Oklahoma prairie clover, trailing phlox (an endangered species), dayflower, leather-flower, catchfly, larkspur, coral bean, yellow wood-sorrel, showy sida, queen's delight, devil's shoestring, Carolina rockrose, butterfly-weed, standing cypress, wild bergamot, spotted beebalm, eastern prickly pear, evening primrose, shaggy portulaca, Texas toad-flax, cup-leaf penstemon, gayfeather, Venus's looking-glass, devil's claw, plains coreopsis, weakstem sunflower, Arkansas lazy daisy, Winkler gaillardia, Reverchon palafoxia, and Hooker palafoxia.

Whoa! Reindeer moss—here in this sweltering sandpile? Sure enough, the great catch-all Big Thicket provides a home to this genera of lichens, known as *Cladonia* to botanists, that serves as a "mainstay in the winter diet of reindeer, lemmings, and other cold-climate animals." So writes Professor C. J. Hylander in *The World of Plant Life.*

Many visitors admire the stately Beech-Magnolia-Loblolly ecosystem most of all.

Explore the following units of the National Preserve for the arid sandylands, as well as the Roy E. Larsen Sandyland Sanctuary:

Hickory Creek Savannah Unit   Beech Creek Unit
Jack Gore Baygall Unit   Turkey Creek Unit
Big Sandy Creek Unit

More on the Larsen Sanctuary in Chapter 9.

Beech-Magnolia-Loblolly

If a vote were taken among first-time visitors to the various ecosystems of the Big Thicket, this one would probably wind up the favorite. It's the classical sylvan beauty.

Large trees spreading over a relatively open forest floor form its most noticeable characteristic. Small, curving creeks often cut their way through the spongy soil. Strange plants and striking mushrooms live here, along with magnificent specimens of hoary azalea abloom in early spring. Their honeysuckle-like perfume at times permeates entire groves of the big trees.

Some ecologists believe that this type of forest is the

ultimate climax natural system in the Big Thicket—the peak of the evolutionary forest scale. Three kinds of trees dominate the environment—the American beech, southern magnolia, and loblolly pine (all described in Chapter 4).

Consider this scenario for the rise, fall, and rise of a climax forest. The final stage of the climax forest would be reached after several hundred years of growth and competition between plants for nutrients and light, undisturbed by human intervention. The three dominant species would eventually eliminate almost all other species competing with them. Probably the last subdominants to go would be white oaks and sugar maples. Then you would have a forest floor of spacious openings between the lordly beeches, magnolias, and loblollies. Lovely herbaceous plants and a selection of hoary azaleas would be permitted to share the cathedral-like area. All processes leading to the climax scene would take place at an extremely gradual pace.

Then, as the climax scene ages in its grandeur, lightning strikes and the forest burns to charred ground. And the long processes would begin again—first, grasses in the clearing, then herbaceous plants followed by shrubs, small "nurse" trees, and the seedlings of giants to come. Acorns of oaks, seeds of hickories, maples, a dozen lesser species, and a new generation of royalty—the seeds of the American beech, southern magnolia, and loblolly pine—would be carried to the spot by birds, wayward winds, and waters. Another climax forest would stir in the kernels toward a time several hundred years ahead.

"Nurse" trees allowed in the neighborhood of the dominants include the redbud, grancy graybead, silver-bell, wild black cherry, hop-hornbeam, toothache tree, muscletree, and dogwood. Major shrubs include hoary azalea and Virginia witch hazel.

In the woods appear Carolina lily, which is rare to uncommon in the Big Thicket, May-apple, wake-robin, Jack-in-the-pulpit, green dragon, and the rare yellow dog's-tooth violet. Orchid species here include whorled pogonia, crippled crane-fly, spring coral-root, and three birds orchid.

Those are just the beginnings. Under the beech trees you find that strange parasite, beech-drops. They grow nowhere else, just under beech trees. They have no chlorophyll—nor does the ghostly Indian pipe found in this ecosystem.

Units of the Big Thicket National Preserve where the Beech-Magnolia-Loblolly realm occurs are:

Beech Creek Unit	Jack Gore Baygall–Neches
Lance Rosier Unit	Bottom Units
Turkey Creek Unit	Upper Neches River Unit
Big Sandy Creek Unit	Beaumont Unit

Cypress Slough

"These are unquestionably the most structurally impressive forest stands in the Big Thicket." So say distinguished ecologists Harcombe and Marks in their definitive work, *Forest Vegetation of the Big Thicket, Southeast Texas.* "In the large stands," they continue, "the trees may reach immense proportions."

Take their word for it. Dr. Harcombe is a faculty member at Rice University and Dr. Marks teaches at Cornell University in New York. Together, they spent summers for several years investigating the biology and ecology of the Big Thicket.

One of the finest examples of the Cypress Slough ecosystem is an easy hour's walk or less—depending on how often you stop to savor the mood of the path—along Kirby Nature Trail. From the Information Station on FM 420, the path leads directly through several other ecosystems to the floodplain of Village Creek and a gorgeous stand of bald cypress trees. The National Park Service has been thoughtful enough to place two benches on the rise overlooking the slough.

Plan to spend some time here, not only gazing at the towering bald cypresses but also inspecting the hundreds of cypress "knees" gnarling out of the mud. You've probably heard a couple of reasons for the picturesque knees. One idea says they help the tree get oxygen to the roots. Another says that the knees bolster the giant tree in the

Enormous cypresses pillar the Cypress Slough ecosystem, this one on the border of Village Creek.

mushy soil, helping to keep it from keeling over. If only one of these theories is right, pick the latter.

Two species of trees dominate the Cypress Slough ecosystem—the bald cypress and the swamp tupelo. Harcombe and Marks point out that the most common swamp-edge tree here is the water hickory. Another abundant tree in the vicinity is water elm. Outside the banks of the slough, you'll find muscle-tree, eastern hop-hornbeam, Carolina ash, red maple, black willow, and the river birch with its conspicuous peeling bark.

Companion shrubs include buttonbush and mock-orange. You'll recognize muscadine grape and rattan-vine twining among the trees.

Among the flowers of the slough, you might spot the lovely Indian-pink, rattlesnake root, cardinal flower, and ladies' tresses orchid, an autumn bloomer.

Where to explore for this ecosystem in the Big Thicket National Preserve:

Turkey Creek Unit Jack Gore Baygall–Neches
Beaumont Unit   Bottom Units
Big Sandy Creek Unit

Watch your step hereabouts. Geraldine Watson, the noted naturalist, observes that the Cypress Slough is a favorite haunt of the water moccasin.

Pine Savannah Wetland

"Nowhere else in our region has the intricate relationship of plants to one another and to their environment achieved such an advanced and delicate balance." So writes Geraldine Watson in her booklet, *Big Thicket Plant Ecology.* And author-photographer-naturalist Geyata Ajilvsgi, in her *Wild Flowers of the Big Thicket,* observes that the wildflowers in this ecosystem include species "of which more than a few are strange and rare." She refers to the four kinds of carnivorous plants found here, and to at least five species of wild orchids, plus the seldom seen bottle-gentian.

"Fossil plants" living here, their species hundreds of millions of years old, include regal fern and club moss.

The delicate Pine Savannah Wetland ecosystem has an open floor dominated by longleaf and loblolly pines.

When you look at a regal fern, you're seeing the same size and form of a plant once brushed by dinosaurs. The club moss, however, used to be as tall as a mature pine tree, but has diminished over the eons to only several inches in height.

Among the youngest species or plants on earth are the carnivorous plants and orchids that grow in the Pine Savannah Wetland, so this is a biological neighborhood of the oldest and youngest living species of earthly plant life, a remarkable community if only for that reason.

Here grow jewels of the wildflower world as well—the grass-pink or Calopogon orchid, yellow-fringed orchid, rose pogonia orchid, snowy orchid, white rose-mallow, yellow sunny-bell, meadow beauty, colic-root, Barbara's buttons, and others. Those strange inhabitants, the carnivorous plants, include the yellow pitcher-plant, butterwort, sundew, and bladderwort.

The widely spaced overstory of this ecosystem combines longleaf and loblolly pines. Under them grow stunted specimens of black gum, sweetgum, and Southern red oak. And under those, sweet-bay magnolia, wax-myrtle, and titi assemble in thick patches creased by grassy meadows. Stagger-bush and Arkansas blueberry dress the borders. Sedges, rushes, and various grasses green the ground.

Many of the plants growing here are finicky about their company. The white rose-mallow, for example, will not be found near the yellow pitcher-plant.

Poor drainage is a chief characteristic of these moist flatlands. Hardpan underlies the soil of closely packed particles of sand.

Fire helps maintain this ecosystem. The indigenous species flourish after a burning. If fire doesn't clean out the area periodically, alien species invade it and choke out the shrub and herbaceous species that belong. The aliens also overwhelm many indigenous wildflowers.

Where to explore for the Pine Savannah Wetlands in the Big Thicket National Preserve:

Hickory Creek Savannah Unit
Turkey Creek Unit
Lance Rosier Unit

Longleaf Pine Upland

There's good news and bad news in the Longleaf Pine Uplands.

Good news first. It's like a big, open, rather unkempt park, this ecosystem, found on the hills and ridges in the northern ranges of the Big Thicket, and sometimes on the mounds of the Pine Wetland Savannahs. Its grassy floors sparkle in spring and summer with wildflowers. What a place for a picnic!

The bad news has several parts. Slash pine has been often overplanted in this ecosystem. Slash is a fast-grower, supplying fodder for the pulpwood mills in minimum time, but overplanting them severely reduces the stands of native wildflowers. Moreover, when skidders remove the pines, the resulting disturbed landscape invites vigorous invader species that crowd out plants belonging here. The

The endangered red-cockaded woodpecker once nested in this typical Longleaf Pine Upland (Champion's Longleaf Pine Hiking Trail, near Chester).

invaders further clog up the open spaces that make this ecosystem so appealing.

Fire is a must to keep the Longleaf Pine Uplands ecologically intact. The invaders perish in fire while indigenous species flourish after the burn.

With its fountain-spray needles, longleaf pine is a dominant species here, along with shortleaf pine, especially where red clay is often packed into the soil. Various oaks may join the pines, and sweetgums may also be found among the taller trees. The natural understory, which will be determined by fire or lack of it, should include dogwood, horse sugar, American holly, red-berried yaupon, red buckeye, and New Jersey tea.

Wildflowers here range from birdfoot violet, slender gayfeather, and puccoon to wine-cup, purple pleat-leaf, rose vervain, Texas Dutchman's-pipe, false foxglove, and the vining Carolina-jessamine. Ferns and mosses provide a harmonizing contrast.

When you see masses of the following plants, you know

the place has been invaded: American beauty-berry, wax-myrtle, flameleaf sumac, southern dewberry, grape vines, and blueberries.

This parklike ecosystem is found in two units of the Big Thicket National Preserve:

Big Sandy Unit   Turkey Creek Unit

Palmetto-Hardwood

Outside the village of Saratoga, to the west, Pine Island Bayou slides south under bridges of FM 770 and through some of the Thicket's best examples of the exotic ecosystem known as Palmetto-Hardwood Flats.

This environment occupies the flattest part of the Big Thicket. It's also the poorest in terms of understory trees and shrubs and ground-cover grasses, yet it's one of the most eye-catching. The palmettos might suggest a tropical retreat, forlorn and abandoned, if it weren't for the stained water of the creeks and debris jutting from the banks.

"In the old days, men rode horses under the palmettos," a folklorist of the area says. "That was before Easterners started paying fancy prices to have the fronds cut and shipped up there for Christmas decorations." The palmetto frond market boomed in the early 1900s. Nowadays, you can still find palmettos ten feet tall in the backlands. They have large trunks, and some botanists say they're not the same species as the smaller palmettos seen from the highway and a few hundred yards inland.

Often standing under several inches of water, the Palmetto-Hardwood environment—possibly the remnant of old levees of ancient rivers—dries up during the hot summer months. Evaporation leaves the clay soil cracked into hard plates.

While the palmetto is the most noticeable plant of this ecosystem, usually standing four to six feet tall in open formation, Harcombe and Marks say the basket oak is the dominant tree. Ajilvsgi assigns that position to the over-cup oak and laurel oak.

Swamp tupelo and bald cypress border the streams. Red maple and sweetgum may be found in numbers; also

The soil of the Palmetto-Hardwood ecosystem alternates between watery and cracked dry.

loblolly pine and Carolina ash. Arrow-wood viburnum is a common shrub. The conspicuous Spanish moss backlit by the sun makes a splendid photograph.

Wildflowers of the area include stinking fleabane, Virginia buttonweed, Missouri ironweed, creeping spot-flower, sharp-sepal penstemon, and eryngium.

Explore this ecosystem in two units of the Big Thicket National Preserve:

Lance Rosier Unit   Loblolly Unit

Oak-Gum Floodplain

"The bottoms"—that's what it's called by old-timers all over the Big Thicket. You'll recognize this ecosystem by its broad forested flats next to the rivers and larger creeks of the Thicket. It soaks under a canopy of sweetgums, oaks, and a dozen or more other kinds of leafy trees. Every year, the Oak-Gum Floodplains undergo flooding by the adjacent waterways. The wonder is that so many tree species not only survive this heavy saturation but thrive on it.

For photographers, the light filtering through the can-

An example of the Oak-Gum Floodplains ecosystem, found on Kirby Nature Trail.

opy often casts an other-worldly effect. One place in the Turkey Creek Unit, near Village Creek, is populated by high numbers of eastern hop-hornbeams and muscle-trees, whose sunlit leaves emit an eerie greenish glow. Few photographers have caught the eeriness on film.

Sweetgum and five oaks dominate this ecosystem, which also harbors basket oak, willow oak, water oak, southern red oak, and overcup oak. Companion trees include Carolina ash, sycamore, alder, river birch, black willow, American holly, water hickory, swamp tupelo, red maple, loblolly pine, and occasionally American beech.

Wildflowers you're apt to find in open areas are lizard's tail, rose-mallow, cardinal flower, and showy sesbania.

Explore these units of the Big Thicket National Preserve for the bottoms:

Beech Creek Unit	Beaumont Unit
Lance Rosier Unit	Upper Neches River Unit
Turkey Creek Unit	Jack Gore Baygall–Neches
Big Sandy Creek Unit	Bottom Units

Mixed-Grass Prairie

This ecosystem is missing from the Big Thicket National Preserve. In fact, it's almost missing now from the entire Big Thicket region. You'll find remnants of Mixed-Grass Prairie between Pine Island Bayou and the Trinity River. You'll also find memories of them in the names of small communities of the area— Batson Prairie, Sam's Prairie, Stockpen Prairie. Pioneers settled early in those places because the ground was already cleared and the soil fertile.

To recognize this ecosystem, look for level, grassy, almost treeless expanses with tall wild grasses, not agricultural grasses. You might also see "pimple mounds," also called "mima mounds," rising several feet high and as much as fifty feet in diameter. Such a mound probably results from a small shrub or clump of grass catching debris from wind or drainage rivulets and over the years building to size. An interesting facet of the mounds is that they become home to plant communities different from those of the surrounding prairies. They have only slightly different soils and elevations, but sufficiently so to attract varying plants and pollinating insects.

Marysee Prairie, located about three miles west of Batson, is called the last virgin prairie of the Big Thicket. Hold the term *virgin* suspect. Most of Marysee has changed into residential development, although seven acres remain in the ownership of a private conservation association.

At this writing those acres are overrun with brush, obliterating the true prairie. Action to clear it and restore the land to its prairie character has begun.

The loss of true prairies in the Thicket can be laid to development, farming, overgrazing, and suppression of fire. Fire was a tool used by Indians to flush game, and by settlers to clear the land of invading species, such as loblolly pine, wax-myrtle, sea myrtle, and various hawthorns.

Naturalists surmise that the Loblolly Unit of the Big Thicket National Preserve, just north of Marysee Prairie, was former virgin prairie overwhelmed by loblollies. Speculation also arises that Pine Island Bayou was a major channel of the Trinity River some eons ago.

Brush and woods encroaching on virgin prairie. Photo of Marysee
Prairie by Maxine Johnston ca. 1979.

Visitors from heartland America will recognize wild
grasses in this Big Thicket ecosystem, as will prairie dwellers from other climes. "Big Thicket prairies are a curious
mixture of vegetation of the Coastal Wetland Prairies,
Central Texas Highland Prairies, and Eastern Tall-grass
Prairies," observes naturalist Geraldine Watson.

Wildflowers bloom all summer long on the prairies—
Kansas gayfeather, prairie bluebell, prairie phlox, winecups,
Indian blanket, herbertia, Carolina rose. Wild grasses include
eastern gamagrass, Indian grass, tall dropseed, various species
of paspalum, panicum, and tridens. Much depends on drainage patterns and the composition of soil—mostly clay or
mostly sand —where the various species grow and flourish.
Different species have different preferences.

One reason this ecosystem isn't represented in the National Preserve is that there wasn't enough of it remaining to qualify for federal management.

River Edge

The National Park Service recognizes the edges of the major waterways in the Thicket as a distinct ecosystem. Harcombe-Marks, Watson, and Ajilvsgi do not mention it. "Black willow and river birch are found on the sandbars throughout the Thicket," commented Dr. Harcombe when told of this classification. "You'll also find sycamores on the levees."

Many species of plants sprout from seeds, uprooted seedlings, and stems that root from nodes, deposited on the river edges by upstream currents or by birds and animals. Whether these sprouts survive is a question of soil stability and other factors. A more detailed description of this "strip environment" should be forthcoming in future studies by the National Park Service. No one doubts its scenic value along the water corridors of the Thicket.

Roadsides

An itinerant puppeteer from the northeast coast drove through the Big Thicket region a few years ago, piloting an old van that seemed more like a piled-up wagon, and looking for places to set up his theater. But he never got around to business. He had happened upon the Thicket in the early springtime, around April Fool's Day, and spent an entire week looking at roadside wildflowers. Then he had to make a gig in Tennessee, so he rambled on.

"No other state can compare with Texas for roadside beauty," he wrote in a letter. "I know, I've been through them all, some a dozen times. But this is a fantasy." He should know. A puppeteer is a fantasy expert.

The springtime roadsides in the Thicket can be glorious. But do they constitute a true ecosystem? Naturalists Watson and Ajilvsgi say yes. So does the National Park Service. Conservative botanists and ecologists are hanging back at the moment. Here's the rationale of the yea-sayers:

At least six factors make the roadsides a distinct ecological reality. One, the plants receive more than usual amounts

32

On the Neches River, a view of a River Edge ecosystem.

of moisture because the adjacent roadway drains on them. Two, the roadsides get far more sunlight and heat than flowers of the woods and parklands receive. Three, the Texas Highway Department mows the roadsides on a regular schedule. Mowing can have either a beneficial or a harmful effect, depending on when and how it's done. Four, the plants of the ecosystems in adjacent fields and forests seed the roadsides, mixing theirs with seeds from other ecosystems dropped by birds, vehicles, and ambling animals. Those strangers might also bring new insects, which might bring new birds, which might bring new bird-eating animals, which might bring a whole new batch of seeds. Five, the road cuts expose plants to a variety of soil types. And six, they're treated to constant doses of herbicides, fumes, and similar offal of today's chemical mania. With all that action, you wonder how they not only survive but look so great in the bargain.

Wildflower displays change during three flowering seasons, beginning in February with redbuds, maples, and yellow jessamine, peaking in the springtime, scaling down but still lovely in summer, and ending with goldenrod and the yellows of autumn.

More people enjoy the roadside ecosystem of the Big Thicket than any other, thanks to highway traffic. Wise travelers also take off down a dirt road or two while on a trip to see what's happening back there.

Either by ignorance or arrogance, some travelers stop by the roadsides and pick bouquets. Most wildflowers wilt within minutes or a few hours after being broken from their stems. Even if they're dug up and replanted, few will survive in strange surroundings, especially while they're putting every atom of their energy into blooming or pollinating and making baby seeds. Since many species of wildflowers are annuals and thereby propagate their kind by seed, the pickers kill that process in an instant.

Leave the flowers be. They'll reproduce new beauties next season.

Sample palettes of the Big Thicket's roadside wildflowers:

Spring—lyre-leaf sage, bluets, violets of many varieties, showy primrose, daisy fleabane, wine-cups, ruellias, brown-eyed Susans, bluebonnets, Drummond phlox, Texas paint-brush, white gaura, self-heal, yellow-flowered composites of many kinds . . .

Summer—yellow-flowered composites of many kinds, Indian blanket, daisies . . .

Autumn—Indian blanket, liatris, viburnum, elderberry, American beauty-berry, goldenrod, clematis, trumpet-creeper, wisteria, passion-flower, Dakota vervain, spider flower, spiderwort . . . and in the roadside ditches, purple pickerel-weed, blue iris, powdery thalia, water-hyacinth, yellow lotus, arrowhead . . .

Ecosystems

It's a safe bet that the rambling puppeteer even had his puppets talking about the roadsides of the Big Thicket. The roadsides lead to even greater treasures in the twelve units of the National Preserve.

3 Units of the National Preserve

Whether you're planning a day's visit to the Thicket, or a week's, or a lifetime's, you need a good map showing the units of the National Preserve. And you're in luck. The National Park Service produces an excellent map of the area in a colorful and informative pocket-fold brochure. This free map is your ticket to tons of outdoor pleasure and discovery.

You're apt to wonder how the units came to be shaped and located in such a manner. The story starts in the 1920s, then picks up in the 1960s. Leaders of the grass-roots movement for a national park or preserve wanted to save representative types of wilderness that make the Big Thicket a world-class biological prize. They had watched, over the decades, nature taking a bad beating from so-called progress and from ignorant or arrogant exploitation.

Washington powers heard proposals to save 400,000 acres of Big Thicket ecosystems. Response: no way. Then 300,000 acres, and the same response. Then 100,000 acres; ditto. The final compromise was 84,550 acres, without two major environs, the Village Creek arid sandylands and the mixed grassland prairies. Nervous during the energy crisis of the early 1970s, Congress insisted that oil and gas exploration be permitted in the Preserve under strict regulations.

Heroes and heroines of those embattled times included Lance Rosier of Saratoga—everyone's inspiration, Alice Cashen and Maxine Johnston of Batson, Geraldine Watson of Silsbee, Dempsie Henley of Liberty, outspoken newspaper editor Archer Fullingim of Kountze, Dr. Pete Gunter of Denton, Harold Nicholas of Saratoga, Orrin and Lorraine Bonney of Houston, Ned Fritz of Dallas, and others. In Congress, the heroes were Senator Ralph W. Yarborough and Congressman Bob Eckhardt. The final legislation would finally be moved through the Washington maze to victory by Congressman Charlie Wilson of Lufkin.

Meanwhile, the units you see now were being largely

Maxine Johnston, a premier leader of "grassroots" conservation movements to preserve Big Thicket areas, takes a break during a Village Creek float.

shaped by the work of Billy Hallmon, a Dallas industrial artist and weekend naturalist, and Maxine Johnston, a university librarian and president of the association of citizens that spearheaded the Save the Big Thicket crusade. On weekends for more than a year, they rambled over the region, poring over property and topographical maps, tramping the woods to mark off desirable ecological areas, excluding family homesteads and developed tracts wherever possible.

"It was Billy's vision to have a plan ready for the National Park Service to consider when, and if, the Preserve

The late Harold Nicholas, self-taught naturalist, primitive artist, and superb field guide. His inscription to me reads, "Where will we go when the Thicket's gone?" Photo by Roy Hamric.

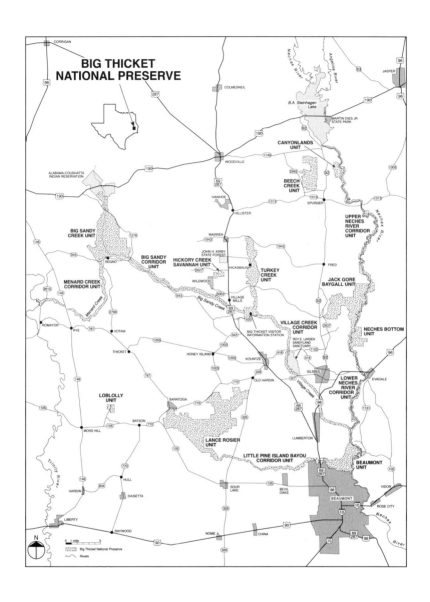

became a reality," Johnston says. When the two completed work on an area, they would ship the maps marked with suggested Preserve boundaries to Congressman Wilson with a request that he ask timber companies to avoid lumbering those areas until Congress made its decision.

So thorough, reasonable, and practical were the recommendations by the Hallmon-Johnston team that they were largely adopted, with some variations, by the National Park Service after its own experts surveyed the ground.

At the time this *Guide* entered its production phase, detailed information on the Preserve's three new units— the Canyonlands Unit and two corridor units—had not been released by the National Park Service. Maps and data on the new units will be available for visitors at Preserve Headquarters and the outlying Ranger Stations after the land is acquired.

Most of the units contain areas of true wilderness quality for future public enjoyment and scientific study. Each unit has a special quality, a special reason for existing. And as guests of nature, all visitors are urged to observe these precautions and good manners:

Don't leave valuables in your car.

Register at the trailhead and take a map.

Take water and insect repellent.

Stay on the trail.

Learn to recognize and avoid poison ivy.

Do not cut or collect plants. They are protected by law.

Detour around snakes. Some are poisonous. All animals are protected.

Avoid bee, wasp, and fire-ant nests.

Do not take wheeled vehicles, pets or horses on the trail, except where horses and bicycles are specifically allowed on the Big Sandy Horse Trail.

Turkey Creek Unit
7,784 Acres

This is the current showpiece unit of the Big Thicket National Preserve. It displays seven ecosystems, tops among the Preserve's fifteen units; more than 70 species of trees; over 50 kinds of wild shrubs; at least 40 varieties of vines . . . and how about 486 known species of herbaceous plants, including 11 orchids and 11 different ferns? That's a conservative tally.

Three well-mapped trails—Kirby Nature Trail, Turkey Creek, and Pitcher Plant Trail—slice and curve through the unit, which is also the site of the projected Big Thicket National Preserve Visitor Center. National Park Service spokespersons say the center will be completed in the latter 1990s. Study a trail map before stepping out. *Units of the National Preserve*

Jagged and skinny in profile, the unit follows a stretch of its namesake creek, and at its southern end sits astride the most comely and popular waterway in the entire region of the Big Thicket, Village Creek.

All these ecosystems gather in this unit: Cypress Slough, Pine Savannah Wetland, Longleaf Pine Upland, Beech-Magnolia-Loblolly, Oak-Gum Floodplain, Arid Sandyland, Baygall. In places some of them will overlap.

Kirby Nature Trail begins at the Information Station on FM 420, 2.5 miles east of the junction of U.S. 69/287 and FM 420. An outer loop extends for 2.4 miles, an inner loop for 1.7 miles. One of the prettiest and most diverse portions of the Big Thicket, this trail should be among the first on the hiking list of every visitor. The inner loop ends on a floodplain pillared by immense bald cypresses. Scores of their knobby "knees" poke through the muck, composing one of the great scenes in the entire Thicket.

Turkey Creek Trail runs north-south for about fifteen miles, paralleling Turkey Creek from FM 1943 to Village Creek. The trailhead on the northern end begins three-and-a-half miles east of Warren on FM 1943. It wiggles about six miles to intersect Hester Bridge Road. If you walk three-plus miles from the trail's beginning, then go eastward for several hundred yards, you'll come to an old road known as Muscadine Road. Now closed, it once bordered beaver ponds. Beavers may still live there, or may have departed, when you read this.

You can also get to the Hester Bridge Road trailhead from the Triple D Guest Ranch. Just take the road from

Park here, at the log-cabin Ranger Station, and stroll along the Kirby Nature Trail for an hour or two.

the ranch eastward for about a half-mile. The trail then meanders southward for three miles to the County Line Road, which cuts through the unit on an east-west line.

From the County Line Road trailhead, the trail leads southward another six miles or so to Sandhill Loop near Village Creek. At Village Creek, an iron bridge connects the Turkey Creek Trail with the Kirby Nature Trail.

Pitcher Plant Trail opens upon a field that may be America's largest expanse of the carnivorous yellow pitcher-plants thriving in the wild. In early April, when the blooming season peaks, the area presents acres of the plant's strange, down-facing flowers aglow in the season's sunlight.

To reach this picturesque area, take FM 1943 eastward from Warren for four miles to a dirt road heading southward. Turn there and drive for two miles to a marked inset at the trailhead. An easy walk of one-quarter mile, all hard surface, takes you to the bridge overlooking the expanse of pitcher-plants. Interpretive signs help visitors understand how the plants trap insects and absorb the flesh.

The overall Turkey Creek Trail spans a remarkable diversity of environments, from sandy pine uplands that

What's around the next bend? This path winds through the Kirby Nature Trail.

have been logged over in recent decades and now show vigorous recovery, to mixed hardwood-evergreen forests, floodplains, and baygalls.

Birds of record in the unit include sharp-shinned hawk, pied-billed grebe, rufous hummingbird, eastern kingbird, brown-headed nuthatch, brown creeper, solitary vireo, black-throated green warbler, blackpoll warbler, ovenbird, Wilson's warbler, scarlet tanager, blue grosbeak, rufous-sided towhee, northern junco, and swamp sparrow.

The seventy-plus species of trees here include American beech and southern magnolia, eight kinds of oaks, four varieties of hawthorns, honey locust, black walnut, white and red mulberry, three native pines and the alien slash pine, and the satin-barked black cherry.

Understory shrubs, numbering at least fifty-two species, include bastard indigo, pawpaw, sea myrtle, downy chinquapin, skunk bush, three different wax-myrtles, and three varieties of wild azaleas.

A few of the forty species of vines: the brilliantly flowering cross-vine, blue jasmine, vase vine, Japanese and coral honeysuckle, and climbing dogbane.

Ferns found here include ebony spleenwort, lady fern, cut grapeleaf fern, rattlesnake fern, chain fern, cinnamon, royal, resurrection, Christmas, southern shield, and Virginia chain fern.

Resident orchids are the Calopogon, coral root, yellow-fringed, small wood orchid, southern tway blade, fragrant ladies' tresses, green-lip ladies' tresses, grass-leaved ladies' tresses, spring ladies' tresses, and crippled crane-fly.

Besides orchids and ferns, the stunning total number of herbaceous species here embraces three carnivorous genera, seven different milkworts, a like number of violets, four skullcaps, six asters, five pipeworts, three lettuces, four dayflowers, and such rarities as the Indian-pink, Carolina-lily, great Solomon's seal, and bottle-gentian. You can find 422 other species, minimum.

And a few of the folklore plants found in this unit: scarlet pimpernel (remember the old adventure movie of that name?) and clasping false pimpernel, screw stem, hairy green-eyes, prairie tea, finger dogshade, purple coneflower,

Take five on a sunlit log in the Turkey Creek Unit.

yerba di tajo, Yankee weed, justice-weed, peppergrass, wild bergamot, three kinds of noseburns, Venus' looking-glass, and bloodroot.

Hickory Creek Savannah Unit
703 Acres

This small unit holds a plethora of nature's delights. Many wildflowers like open spaces and moisture, so they abound here. Raccoons and coyotes make part of their living in these environs, along with proliferating armadillos. Interesting trees, shrubs, and grasses provide cover.

The National Park Service has built a long bridge for easy access to the savannah's attractions. The bridge also protects the extremely delicate plants from being damaged or destroyed by human foot traffic. A first rule for visitors: Stay on the bridge.

Two loops comprise the Sundew Trail, as it's called after one of the most numerous carnivorous plants in residence. The short loop extends for one-quarter mile from the trailhead; it's wheelchair accessible. The outer trail covers a one-mile-long loop.

Three ecosystems pattern this unit: Pine Savannah Wetland, Arid Sandyland, and Baygall.

Among the birds you might spot in Hickory Creek Savannah are painted bunting, northern junco, blue grosbeak, prairie warbler, black-throated green warbler, brown-headed nuthatch, sharp-shinned hawk, great horned owl, eastern kingbird, and the rare and endangered red-cockaded woodpecker.

A checklist shows twenty-eight species of trees here, including seven that flower in the springtime: red maple, grancy graybeard, flowering dogwood, mayhaw, titi, sassafras, and sweetleaf or horse-sugar, so called in folklore because of its faint sweetness of foliage to the tongue.

Of the recorded thirty-two species of wild shrubs, six put forth showy flowers—hoary azalea, low white azalea, tall white azalea, arrow-wood viburnum, possum-haw viburnum, and Louisiana yucca.

Twenty-four kinds of vines made the checklist for this unit, including eight beauties: net-leaf leather-flower, Carolina-jessamine, Japanese honeysuckle, trumpet-creeper, and purple and yellow passion-flower.

Plant experts have identified at least 310 species of herbaceous plants here, about half of which produce showy flowers in season. They include three kinds of gayfeather—pinkscale, Kansas, and sharp; four species of meadow beauty—rose, yellow, Maryland, and common; and six orchid species—yellow-fringed, snowy, bearded grass-pink, grass-pink, rose pogonia, and spring ladies' tresses.

Ferny folks will pick out at least seven kinds of their favorites: royal, cinnamon, chain, Christmas, bracken, Virginia chainfern, and resurrection. The meat-eaters include sundews, yellow bladderworts, and yellow pitcher-plants. Folklore plants here include nettle-leaved noseburn and two of its relatives, Small's noseburn and wavy-leaved noseburn, and three kinds of cudweed—purple, common, and fragrant.

To get to the Hickory Creek Savannah and its Sundew Trail, take U.S. 69/287 to FM 2827, turn west, slow down, and take the first left to the trailhead.

The yucca depends on the yucca moth for pollination and propagation;
the moth depends on the plant for food. A symbiotic relationship.

One of the Thicket's most beautiful wild orchids, the May-blooming Calopogon. Thoreau wrote of its grace and loveliness.

Jack Gore Baygall and Neches Bottom Units
13,314 Acres Combined

"Jack Gore Baygall is about three miles wide and four miles long, a jungle-like region for the most part where sunlight filters through 100-foot-tall tupelos and cypresses to reach the thick undergrowth in eerie green shafts. By night the sounds of animals moving, calling, warning others of their kind, fill the recesses of the baygall. It's the home of alligators, otters, beavers, hawks, owls, roadrunners, snakes, fox squirrels, and whitetail deer. It once reverberated with the roars of bears and the howls of panthers. Oaks growing out of the muck to heights of 135 feet sprouted from acorns in the days when America was a British colony. The Jack

A neighborhood of one of earth's most primitive plants, royal fern, and one of the most recent to appear on the evolutionary scale, the carnivorous yellow pitcher plant, in a Big Thicket seep.

Gore Baygall is a wild piece of the Big Thicket National Preserve."

So I wrote some years ago for a book about the Big Thicket. The mood expressed in that observation hasn't changed much over the generations, if at all, particularly at twilight. The National Park Service survey in 1979 expressed the view that 11,000 acres of Jack Gore Baygall and the Neches Bottom Unit had long-range potential to qualify as true wilderness.

To experience that feeling, you need to get beyond the oil field and pipeline operations in the western chunk of the Jack Gore Baygall Unit. The Timber Slough Road will take you past the pumpers. Running east-west across the top of the Jack Gore Baygall Unit, it ends at a beautiful sandbar on the Neches River—if the sandbar hasn't been rivered away by the time you get there. You might have to hike about three miles from the parking area on Timber Slough Road, over Black Creek, to the Neches River sandbar, for the road often won't accommodate autos or trucks after a bad spell of weather. Ask ahead.

Besides the biggest baygall anywhere around, the complex of Jack Gore Baygall Unit and Neches Bottom Unit encompasses these ecosystems: Oak-Gum Floodplain, Beech-Magnolia-Loblolly, Cypress Slough, and—surprisingly—Arid Sandyland.

Among the birds of this area are the tricolored heron, black-bellied whistling duck, spotted sandpiper, northern rough-winged swallow, and warbling vireo.

You've got access to both units from FM 2937, which takes off from FM 92 at several points between Silsbee and Fred. Neches Bottom Unit contains a county park. Jack Gore Baygall Unit contains three lakes—John's, Franklin, and Sally Withers. Your Big Thicket brochure map shows them all.

This unit was named after the son of a North Carolina foot-racer and bare-knuckle fighter, known as Grandpa Gore, who found his way to the Big Thicket from Alabama several years before the Civil War. He had been advised to leave Alabama after winning a ferocious battle with an eye-gouger and ear-biter who threatened to take Grandpa

Timber Slough Road cuts across the top of Jack Gore Baygall and ends near the Neches River. Look out for bad weather washouts.

Gore to court if and when he, the loser, healed. Grandpa's son, Jack, was a farmer, cattleman, and hunter. Jack's son, Stanley, once described the baygall thus:

"It's so thick that nothing don't travel in it much. It's just solid water in places. You would bog down in mud and water. It's a terrible place."

To some travelers, yes. To others, a dark and different delight.

Beech Creek Unit
5,089 Acres

Looking for a bit of solitude? This may be your spot. A loop trail winds through sections of deep forest here, and if you're alone, you'll probably have no more company than the sights and sounds of the woods and your own thoughts.

Other parts of the Beech Creek Unit need time to recover from long years of timber-cutting. And in the 1970s, the pine bark beetle thinned out large sections of pines, leaving whitened trunks in their wake. Nature reclaims such areas, and that's the process taking place now. Birds, deer, and mammals appreciate the young, vigorous growth, though to human values, these areas often appear messy, even wrecked.

The future of this unit holds great promise. A National Park Service survey several years ago found 4,800 acres to be a "wilderness objective area," meaning that the area has a long-range potential for true wilderness.

You can observe four ecosystems here: Beech-Magnolia-Loblolly, Oak-Gum Floodplain, Baygall, and Arid Sandylands.

Birds to be spotted in this unit: Mississippi kite, sharp-shinned hawk, long-eared owl, bank swallow, brown-headed nuthatch, Bewick's wren, solitary vireo, black-throated green warbler, rose-breasted grosbeak, ovenbird, and the endangered red-cockaded woodpecker.

Trees: at least fifty-four species, including two kinds of maples, seven oaks, two ashes, the devil's walking stick and toothache tree, three hickories, and the alternate-leaf dogwood as well as the flowering dogwood.

Pioneers used the inner bark of the "toothache tree" to lessen pain
of sore gums or tooth problems. It's also called "tingletongue."

Wild shrubs: at least thirty-eight species, including four
kinds of hollies, two witch hazels, the he-huckleberry and
ungendered huckleberry, stagger-bush, fetter-bush, three
kinds of blueberries, and four varieties of viburnum.

You'll see twenty-nine kinds of vines, from eardrop-
vine to hairy cluster-vine to sarsaparilla-vine and Atlantic
yam, bull-brier, yellow and purple passion-flowers.

How about 169 species of herbaceous plants, minimum?
That includes 64 plants with showy flowers in their various seasons, a forest floor purpled with seven violets—
primrose-leaf, bayou, trilobed, Walter's, Missouri, and
lance-leaved.

Eight kinds of ferns live here: lady fern, cut grapeleaf
fern, Southern shield, chain fern, sensitive, cinnamon, royal,

Beech trees have a distinctive way of embracing their home soil.

and Christmas. You've got coral-root and southern tway-blade orchids to identify. The fact that no one has officially recorded the crippled crane-fly orchid here amazes me.

Besides the above artworks, this unit contains such interesting folklore dwellers as the nits-and-lice plant, nodding nixie, tooth-cup, pony foot and elephant toes, poor Joe, stinking fleabane, beefsteak plant, blue curls, the short-peduncled snoutbean, and heal-all.

To reach this unit, find Spurger on your map, about seven miles south of B. A. Steinhagen Lake. West of Spurger on FM 1013, not quite three miles, FM 2992 shoots north. About 1.9 miles north of the intersection, you'll see a sign directing you to the trailhead.

The Beech Creek Unit verges on becoming a star part of the Big Thicket National Preserve. Give it time to regenerate. Meanwhile, watch that fascinating process and enjoy the tree-canopied Beech Creek Trail now. It's a natural for solitude.

Big Sandy Creek Unit
14,346 Acres

This unit rivals the Turkey Creek Unit for diversity and richness of natural endowments, and boasts its own distinctions as well.

Horse riders appreciate the fact that they've got a long

trail here for enjoying parts of the National Preserve in their own style—astride their mounts. Big Sandy is the only unit of the Preserve where horses are permitted. The same goes for bicycle enthusiasts. But no motorized bikes are permitted in the unit—only those moved by muscle.

One of the three developed trails in this unit circles a series of beaver ponds. Named the Beaver Slide Trail, it loops for a mile-and-a-half around ponds dammed up a while back by the tooth-and-tail engineers. To reach Beaver Slide Trail, find FM 943 running through Segno on the southern edge of the Big Sandy Creek Unit. About three miles east of Segno is the trailhead.

The Big Sandy Creek Horse Trail makes an eighteen-mile round-trip ride, beginning on the Sunflower Road three miles west of Dallardsville. An excellent trail for hiking as well as for horseback riding and bicycling, it roams through uplands, slopes, and floodplains. It passes abandoned oil-drilling sites, now recovering their natural state, and a fine beaver pond of its own. Volunteers cleared this special trail in several summers of strenuous work periods beginning in 1986.

The National Park Service has established nine rules and regulations for riding horseback in this unit, including "horses must be kept under physical control at all times; they may not be left to graze or water unattended," and "horses must not be tied closer than 100 feet to any stream or water source." Riders should obtain the complete regulations from the National Park Service headquarters or a ranger station.

At the northern prong of the Big Sandy Creek Unit, a third trail, the Woodlands, reveals a mix of past human uses of the area with expanses of natural habitats. The trailhead is on FM 1276, 3.3 miles south of the intersection of U.S. 190. Covering almost five-and-a-half miles, the trail skirts an old pond built by a onetime rancher, makes way through a grassy area, drops into the floodplains of Big Sandy Creek, follows the path of this pretty creek to up-slopes of Beech-Magnolia-Loblolly pine woods, and tracks a boundary line of the Alabama-Coushatta Indian Reservation.

Units of the National Preserve

A path in the company of giants in the upper Big Thicket of Tyler County.

The eastern leg at the top of the loop follows the flood-plain of Big Sandy Creek. Warning: look out for standing water. Big Sandy might overflow its banks at any time of the year, obscuring the trail in such a way that you could easily get lost if you attempted to hike it. Moreover, you could step into a deep hole hidden by the water and break or sprain a leg or ankle.

You'll find six rich ecosystems in the Big Sandy Creek Unit—Cypress Slough, Beech-Magnolia-Loblolly, Baygall, Oak-Gum Floodplain, Longleaf Pine Upland, and Arid Sandyland.

More than four hundred species of herbaceous plants intrigue botanist and plant-people here. Among the wild orchids: fragrant ladies' tresses, ragged fringed orchid, southern twayblade, small wood orchid, grass-leaved ladies' tresses, and crippled crane-fly orchid. Ferns abound—ebony spleenwort, lady fern, cut grapeleaf, rattlesnake fern, Florida shield fern, southern shield fern, chain, cinnamon, royal, resurrection, Christmas, bracken, and Virginia chain fern.

Folklore plants include colic-root, beggars lice, rattle-snake-weed, tobacco weed, boneset, wartweed, self-heal, Indian-turnip, tuckahoe, blackberry and dewberry, and those salad delights, curly dock and sow thistle. Those are only the beginnings. Also, you have Jack-in-the-pulpit, three Dutchman's-pipes—Texas, Virginia, and woolly; eight tick clovers—little, smooth, sand, Maryland, tall, panicled, pine barren, and green; five bedstraws—catchweed, woods, hairy, marsh, and fragrant; three cudweeds—purple, fragrant, and plain cudweed; three flaxes—toad, sucker, and plain; the ghostly Indian-pipe and exclusive beech drop; carnivorous sundews and yellow bladderwort; and the storied May-apple or mandrake.

Tree experts have tallied seventy-six species of trees in this unit, from devil's walking stick to two-winged silver-bells, from chinquapin to cigar-tree, and eight kinds of oak.

Wild shrubs: at least fifty-two species, including red buckeye, Eve's necklace, and five kinds of small hollies—Carolina, baygall, possum-haw, Georgia, and yaupon.

Lacing the trees and shrubs are forty-two species of vines, from American potato-bean to wisteria.

The rare and beleaguered red-cockaded woodpecker nests (or has nested) here, sharing the food supply with the great horned owl, eastern kingbird, brown-headed nuthatch, rufous-sided towhee, and northern junco . . . among other winged visitors and residents.

A suggestion that the unit be named in honor of former Senator Ralph W. Yarborough, a hero of the Save the Big Thicket movement, was declined. The philosopher-fighter-statesman deferred to the natural definer of the environment, the beautiful creek itself.

Lance Rosier Unit
24,942 Acres

This unit comes as close to containing hallowed ground as any in the Big Thicket. It was the home territory of the modest, self-taught naturalist who inspired the national movement of grass-roots citizens to save remnants of the Big Thicket for posterity.

Lance Rosier's field trips into the woods near his home at Saratoga, and elsewhere in the lower Big Thicket region, became the stuff of legend. Into the wonders of plant life, bird life, all animal life, he led school groups, club groups, scientists, artists, writers, foresters, photographers, high-level public officials, passersby, tourists, virtually anyone with an open mind and heart who came his way. His most famous student on the path was U.S. Supreme Court Justice William O. Douglas, who helped to immortalize Rosier in his book, *Farewell to Texas,* and gave an immense nationwide push to the Save the Big Thicket crusade.

Rosier lived his entire life in the town of Saratoga, which borders a part of the unit. There he taught himself botany and zoology from books borrowed from the public library. By lamplight and field trips, he mastered not only the recognition and habitats of hundreds of native species but also their scientific names. He wanted to discuss them with scientists, and he knew scientists used the Latin and Greek names of plants to be certain of identity. His protégé, the late Harold Nicholas, became one of the great

guides of the Thicket in the late 1960s and 1970s, the cru-
cial years of building support for a national park or preserve. Nicholas not only served as an indispensable guide
during that period, but also revealed a striking talent for
painting primitive watercolors of wildflowers.

Big Thicket legends grew like weeds out of the woods
bounded by this unit—legendary bear hunts of the Hooks
brothers in the early 1900s and oil-boom high jinks following the Saratoga strike in 1902. Just north of the town,
splitting off of FM 787, another legend formed on the
Ghost Road, officially the Bragg Road. Parked lovers and
other trustworthy witnesses say they've seen balls of "ghost
light," about the size of a man's decapitated head, skitter-
ing through the woods on that lonely seven-mile red dirt
straightaway.

Oilfields dot the western knob of the unit, south of
Saratoga, and portions of the northeast section as well.
Despite those operations, the unit contains large wilderness areas, including the oldest baygall in the Big Thicket.
A 1979 government survey estimated that 24,000 acres have
the long-range potential for true wilderness. By far the
largest unit in the Big Thicket National Preserve, the Lance
Rosier Unit can be explored along several roads. You'll find
a trailhead off of FM 326, about three miles south of the
intersection with FM 770. Several dirt roads serve as trails
and connect in the area, which was the bear-hunting territory of Ben and Bud Hooks, of Kountze.

Another area to explore lies east of Saratoga, where an
oilfield road leads south for a short distance before inter-
secting with the Cotton Road, which angles eastward. Lance
Rosier's homesite is located at the end of Cotton Road. In
that region, Rosier spotted one of the last specimens of the
ivory-billed woodpecker seen in North America. Larger
than the pileated woodpecker, which it resembles in some
respects, the ivory-billed flew with a two-foot wing span.

This unit harbors a marvelous diversity of plants and
wildlife in five ecosystems: Baygall, Beech-Magnolia-Loblolly, Oak-Gum Floodplain, Palmetto-Hardwood, and Pine
Savannah Wetland. Some of the Thicket's largest sweet-bay
magnolias and swamp tupelos live here. Among the birds

Legends abound about the Old Ghost Road near Saratoga.

recorded in the Unit are the painted bunting, blue grosbeak, brown-headed nuthatch, prairie warbler, and eastern king-bird. Checklists of its myriad species of trees, shrubs, vines, and herbaceous plants remain to be compiled.

Beaumont Unit
5,955 Acres

Talk about low and wet! This place is almost out of sight. It's the lowest and wettest unit of the whole Big Thicket National Preserve. Most of it can be best enjoyed by boat, although several rises hold appeal for folks who crave solid footing. One of those rises, called Lakeview Sand Bar, makes a superb place for riverside lollygagging. It's located on the east bank of the Neches River at a turnoff from FM 1131, north of Vidor.

A good way to view typical scenes of the unit is to make reservations for one of the canoe trips organized by the National Park Service.

Wildlife gathers in variety and abundance in the Beaumont Unit because of its relatively sparse human traffic

60

and its abundance of water and nesting sites. It has sanctuary quality. Nearly surrounded by water, the unit's southern border is the plain of Pine Island Bayou, its eastern border the plain of the Neches River, and much of its northern border the Lower Neches Valley Authority canal. A wedge of about 560 acres of land spreads to Pine Island Bayou, completing the perimeters. Cook's Lake, a popular boating spot, is located about a half-mile west of the junction of Pine Island Bayou and Neches River.

On the raised slopes of this unit, you'll find the Beech-Magnolia-Loblolly ecosystem. On lower elevations—and we're talking just a few feet lower—you'll find Oak-Gum Floodplain and Cypress Slough ecosystems. Some of the cypress trees in the sloughs present fantasy forms. One ancient tree with a partially hollowed base reveals forms that have given it the name "Madonna Cypress." The onetime national champion black hickory *(Carya texana)* tree was found in this unit.

Tricolored heron, mottled duck, and ruddy turnstone are birds of special interest recorded in the Beaumont Unit.

Loblolly Unit
550 Acres

If you've got some detective in your blood, you might take an eye-narrowed interest in this unit. Some ecologists think it's changing from a onetime prairie to a future hardwood forest. If so, the huge loblolly pines here represent a transitional phase. That phase of a forest strongly appeals to studious naturalists, who are always trying to detect signs of the past phase—in this case, prairie—and signs of the oncoming phase, a hardwood forest. To make exploring easy, a county road running north and south cuts through the unit.

Stands of large loblollies and water-loving oaks catch your attention here. But it's not the prettiest place in the National Preserve. A while back, pine bark beetles hit it hard. After days of rain, the ground may hold inches of water, a condition that creates superb reflections for photographs on sunshiny days.

This unit supports at least thirty-nine species of trees, from persimmon to slippery elm and eight kinds of oak; ten species of wild shrubs; nineteen varieties of vines; and ninety-five herbaceous species, including more than thirty wildflowers and six kinds of ferns. Orchid-spotters discover the coral-root and southern twayblade here. Palmettos spread out in large patches under the hardwoods, tipping off the name of the ecosystem prevailing in the unit: Palmetto-Hardwood.

Two of the Thicket's most flamboyant birds, the painted bunting and the scarlet tanager, alight here. The tanager comes in the spring. The bunting arrives in spring and stays through fall, according to records. Other birds on the official lists include the brown creeper and blue-winged warbler.

To get to the Loblolly Unit, take Texas 105 out of Batson, going west. Drive about 2.6 miles and you'll see a road running to your right, or north. follow that road to another right-turning road, which will take you into the unit.

The Corridor Units

Water is the lifeblood of the Big Thicket, and its natural supply must be assured for the Thicket to evolve and flourish. Five slender corridors of water supply have been designated to receive permanent protection, along with the vegetation of their floodplains.

From Dam B to the Jack Gore Baygall and Neches Bottom Units, the Upper Neches River Corridor consists of 4,744 acres averaging less than 1,000 feet in width. Boat access facilities are located below Dam B and at the point where the county highway crosses the unit.

From the Neches Bottom Unit to the Beaumont Unit, the Lower Neches Corridor consists of 2,597 acres averaging less than 1,500 feet in width.

A rich bird life frequents these stretches of the Neches River and environs. Among the birds of record are the American white pelican, ring-billed gull, Franklin's gull, Caspian tern, Forster's tern, black tern, American swallow-tailed kite, spotted sandpiper, northern rough-winged swallow, barn swallow, tricolored heron, and black-bellied whistling duck. On the Upper Neches Corridor, bird-watchers have sighted the bald eagle.

On the northwestern edge of the Preserve area, the Menard Creek Corridor consists of 3,805 acres south of the Big Sandy Creek Unit to its confluence with the Trinity River. The average width figures less than 1,000 feet. Motors no larger than five horsepower are allowed on boats here.

From the Lance Rosier Unit eastward to the Beaumont Unit, the Little Pine Island Bayou Corridor Unit includes 2,209 acres averaging less than 1,000 feet in width. Again, motorboats are limited to a maximum of five horsepower on this water corridor.

Similar data on the two new corridors, the Big Sandy Creek Corridor Unit and the Village Creek Corridor Unit, except for acreage, had not been compiled or released by the National Park Service when this *Guide* went to press.

Definition of Wilderness
from Public Law 88–577, "The Wilderness Act"

"A wilderness, in contrast with those areas where man and his own works dominate the landscape, is hereby recognized as an area where the earth and its community of life are untrammeled by man, where man himself is a visitor who does not remain.

"An area of wilderness is further defined to mean in this Act an area of undeveloped Federal land retaining its primeval character and influence . . . protected and managed so as to preserve its natural conditions and which (1) generally appears to have been affected primarily by the forces of nature, with the imprint of man's work substantially unnoticeable; (2) has outstanding opportunities for solitude or a primitive and unconfined type of recreation . . . and may also contain ecological, geological, or other features of scientific, educational, scenic or historical value."

4 Tips on Identifying Dominant Trees

This chapter points out conspicuous features of the twenty-four dominant trees mentioned in Chapter 2 on "Ecosystems of the Big Thicket." For complete, detailed scientific descriptions of a species, the reader should consult a botanical authority such as *Trees of East Texas,* by Robert A. Vines. The tips here are meant to help newer naturalists get a start on tree identifications.

Although only a few species here get their flowers mentioned—those particular flowers being a major factor in recognizing certain trees—the reader should be mindful that all trees have flowers. They come in male and female genders. Some kinds of trees produce both sexes on the same tree, perhaps to make pollination easier, while other species, such as the hollies, separate the sexes. Most trees have inconspicuous flowers, but some naturalists make a special effort in the spring to note them.

All the dominants in this chapter are deciduous, losing their leaves in winter and regrowing foliage in the spring, except the three pines, the southern magnolia, gallberry holly, and laurel oak. The latter isn't botanically categorized as an evergreen, but in the Big Thicket region it keeps a goodly number of its leaves throughout the winter.

Leaf Types

Refer to the drawings titled Twigs and Leaves, and Leaf Shapes for understanding terms used in leaf descriptions. Drawings from Texas Forest Service Bulletin No. 20.

Sweet-bay Magnolia
Magnolia virginiana

Preferred habitat: baygalls
Also called: white-bay magnolia
Height—to 90 feet. Bark—light gray. Branchlets are silky

TWIGS AND LEAVES

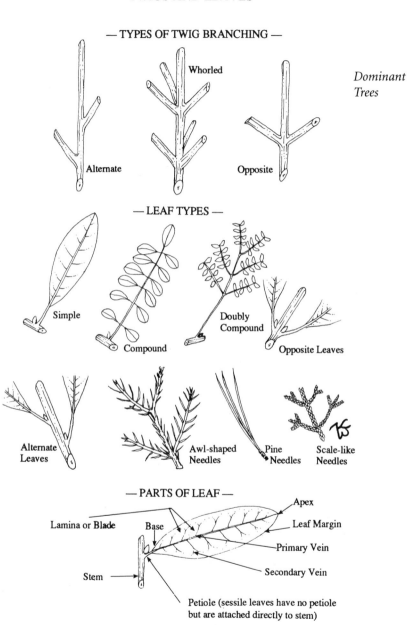

— TYPES OF TWIG BRANCHING —

Whorled

Dominant
Trees

Alternate

Opposite

— LEAF TYPES —

Simple

Compound

Doubly
Compound

Opposite Leaves

Alternate
Leaves

Awl-shaped
Needles

Pine
Needles

Scale-like
Needles

— PARTS OF LEAF —

Apex

Lamina or Blade   Base

Leaf Margin

Primary Vein

Secondary Vein

Stem

Petiole (sessile leaves have no petiole
but are attached directly to stem)

LEAF SHAPES

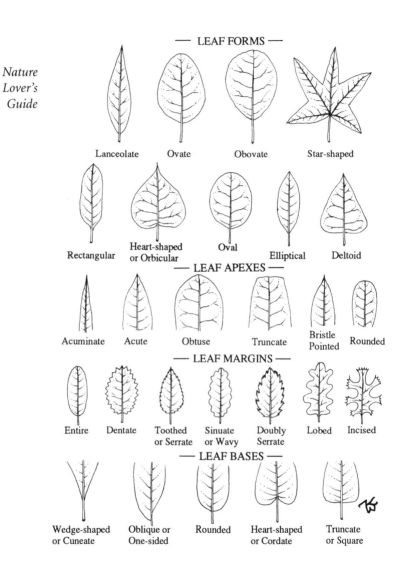

— LEAF FORMS —

Lanceolate   Ovate   Obovate   Star-shaped

Rectangular   Heart-shaped or Orbicular   Oval   Elliptical   Deltoid

— LEAF APEXES —

Acuminate   Acute   Obtuse   Truncate   Bristle Pointed   Rounded

— LEAF MARGINS —

Entire   Dentate   Toothed or Serrate   Sinuate or Wavy   Doubly Serrate   Lobed   Incised

— LEAF BASES —

Wedge-shaped or Cuneate   Oblique or One-sided   Rounded   Heart-shaped or Cordate   Truncate or Square

white. Leaves—4–6 inches long, 1–2 inches wide; simple, oblong; pale green above, white and hairy beneath. Flowers— 9–12 creamy white petals, about 3 inches wide; Fragrant. Fruit—oval-shaped aggregate, brown or dark red, about 2 inches long, bearing scarlet seeds ½ inch long. Clues—the showy white undersides of the leaves, and the lovely flowers, which aren't as big or as showy as the southern magnolia's but are plenty pretty on their own.

This tree is a dominant species in the Baygall ecosystem and appears elsewhere in the Big Thicket region.

Gallberry Holly
Ilex coriacea

Preferred habitat: baygalls
Also called: large gallberry, baygall-bush
Height—usually a shrub, to 15 feet. Bark—smooth, tight-fitting, mottled gray or brown. Leaves—dark green above, stiff, evergreen; about 1½–2 inches long; simple, alternate; often elliptic or obovate in shape. Fruit—black, shiny, rounded drupe. Clue—often grows in crowded colonies in baygalls and other very wet places.

This species is a dominant in the Baygall ecosystem and appears elsewhere in the Big Thicket region.

Bluejack Oak
Quercus incana

Preferred habitat: dry sandhills
Also called: sandjack oak
Height—to 25 feet. Bark—divided into squarish blocks 1–2 inches long and covered with dark scales tipped with red. Leaves—2–5 inches long, 1½ inches wide; yellow midrib; oblong-lanceolate in shape; pale blue-green above, whitish beneath. Flowers—reddish, appearing in spring. Fruit—acorns about ½ inch long, rounded at ends.

This tree is a dominant species in portions of the Arid Sandylands ecosystem and appears elsewhere in the Big Thicket region.

Post Oak
Quercus stellata

Preferred habitat: poor upland soils
Height—to 50 feet. Rounded crown. Bark—reddish brown, divided by deep fissures into scaly ridges. Leaves—distinctively five-lobed, 4–5 inches long, nearly as broad; leathery; dark green above, lighter and hairy below. Fruit—oval-shaped acorn, ½–1 inch long. Small, scaly cup. Clue—leaf shape reminds some people of the Iron Cross.

This tree is a dominant species in portions of the Arid Sandylands ecosystem and appears elsewhere in the Big Thicket region.

Shortleaf Pine
Pinus echinata

Preferred habitat: upland tracts
Also called: short straw pine, silkwood pine
Height—to 100 feet. Bark—brownish red, broken into rectangular plates. Leaves—needles, 3–5 inches long; dark blue-green, clusters of two or three. Flowers—pale purple, cluster at base of new leaf growth. Fruit—smallish cone, 1½–2½ inches wide. Clues—"Ping-Pong ball"–size cones, shorter leaves than other native species.

The shortleaf pine is a dominant species in portions of the Arid Sandylands ecosystem and in the Longleaf Pine Uplands ecosystem. It occurs randomly in the Big Thicket region.

Southern Red Oak
Quercus falcata

Preferred habitat: dry uplands; also moist soils
Also called: Spanish oak, turkey oak, turkey-foot oak
Height—to 80 feet. Bark—varies from light gray on young trees to dark gray or nearly black on older trees; rough, with shallow fissures. Leaves—lobes tipped with bristles, often irregularly shaped but usually pointed. Underside is brown or gray. Fruit—pairs of rounded acorns about ½ inch long in saucer-shaped cups; bitter to the taste. Clue—leaves can remind observer of turkey foot imprint.

Southern red oak is a dominant species in portions of

the Arid Sandylands ecosystem and the Oak-Gum Flood-plains ecosystem. It occurs randomly in the Big Thicket region.

Longleaf Pine
Pinus palustris

Preferred habitat: sandy soils
Also called: southern yellow pine, Georgia pine
Height—to 120 feet. Bark—orange-brown, furrowed, broken into thinnish scales. Leaves—needles, gray-green; 10–15 inches long; in clusters of three, spraying fountain-like from ends of twigs. Flowers—rosy purple, appear in early spring before new leaves. Fruit—a large cone, 6–12 inches or more in length; curved, small prickles on thick scales. Clues—long, "fountain-spray" needles. Larger cone than other native pines.

Longleaf pine is a dominant species in three ecosystems: Longleaf Pine Upland, Pine Savannah Wetland, and portions of the Arid Sandylands. It occurs on other sites in the Big Thicket region.

Loblolly Pine
Pinus taeda

Preferred habitat: moist sites, old fields
Also called: old-field pine
Height—to 120 feet. Bark—brownish to rusty colored and rather dark; deeply furrowed; sometimes 2 inches thick on large trees. Leaves—needles 6–9 inches long, usually three to a cluster but sometimes two. Flowers—bright yellow clusters appearing in spring. Fruit—a cone 3–6 inches long.

Loblolly pine is a dominant species in three ecosystems: Beech-Magnolia-Loblolly, Pine Savannah Wetland, and portions of the Arid Sandylands. It occurs abundantly throughout the Big Thicket region.

White Oak
Quercus alba

Preferred habitat: high-quality soils
Height—to 80 feet. Bark—ash gray, with loose scales or

plates. Leaves—5–9 inches long, deeply divided into five or nine rounded lobes; young leaves often reddish or silvery; colorful in fall. Fruit—acorn about 1 inch long; light brown; partially enclosed in warty cup; considered a "sweet" acorn, relished by wildlife. Clues—scaly, ashy bark; leaves with finger-like lobes.

This tree is a dominant species in portions of the Arid Sandylands ecosystem and a codominant in certain mixed hardwood-evergreen forests. It appears throughout the Big Thicket region. This species holds high rank among trees in American history; white oak timbers were used to construct Old Ironsides, the U.S.S. *Constitution.* Big Thicket pioneers sought it as an indicator of rich soil, suitable for making quick crops.

Blackjack Oak
Quercus marilandica

Preferred habitat: dry, sandy, gravelly, poor soils
Height—to 60 feet. Bark—rough, dark, blocky; inner bark orange or yellowish. Leaves—4–10 inches long; leathery; dark green above, lighter green below; usually wedge-shaped but the shape varies. Fruit—acorn about ¾-inch long, yellow-brown, often striped. Cup covers half the acorn's body.

This tree is a dominant species in portions of the Arid Sandylands ecosystem and appears elsewhere in the Big Thicket region.

Black Hickory
Carya texana

Preferred habitat: sandy uplands
Height—to 75 feet. Bark—dark gray to nearly black; divided into rough ridges, sometimes separated into thin scales. Leaves —8–12 inches long; usually has seven leaflets but sometimes five; shiny dark green above, paler below; rusty brown hairs on petioles of young leaves. Fruit— sweet-kernel nut about 1¼ inches long, obovoid in shape. Clue—the rusty-brown hairs on young leaves and branches.

Black hickory is a dominant species in portions of the

Arid Sandylands ecosystem and occurs in other locations in the Big Thicket region.

American Beech
Fagus grandifolia

Preferred habitat: stream bottomlands
Height—to 120 feet. Bark—light gray with dark mottling; tight-fitting sheath. Leaves—3–4 inches long; simple, alternate, pointed at tip; coarsely toothed and hairy along margin; very bright green when they first appear in spring, turning dark green in summer, golden in fall, rosy brown in winter. Fruit—three-sided nut, borne in pairs; brownish, sweet kernel; a favorite food of wildlife. Clues—smooth sheath of gray bark; trunk often has hollows; roots begin above ground, seeming to embrace the earth; the green of springtime leafing appears electric in sunlight.

Dominant Trees

This tree is a dominant species in the Beech-Magnolia-Loblolly ecosystem, and appears elsewhere in the Big Thicket region. Considered one of America's most beautiful trees in any season.

Southern Magnolia
Magnolia grandiflora

Preferred habitat: moist soil
Height—to 80 feet. Bark—brownish gray, covered with thin scales. Leaves—5–8 inches long; thick, leathery; dark green and shiny above, rust colored on underside, occasionally silvery on underside. Flowers—the most spectacular in the American forest; 6–8 inches wide; creamy white petals splashed in the center with maroon or purple; superb fragrance; appear May–June. Fruit—egg-shaped aggregate 3–4 inches long, bearing scarlet seeds on the surface. The fruit releases each seed on a thin string, on which the seed can swing in the breeze before dropping. Clues—the exceptional flower; the rust-colored underside of the leaves.

This tree is a dominant species in the Beech-Magnolia-Loblolly ecosystem and appears in yards as well as in the wild in the Big Thicket region. The South's best-known tree.

Bald Cypress
Taxodium distichum

Preferred habitat: swamps, sloughs
Also called: southern cypress
Height—to 130 feet. Bark—cinnamon red to gray or silvery, finely divided by vertical fissures. Leaves—light green, ½–¾ inch long; set feather-like on two sides of branchlets; turning rust-colored in fall. Unlike most conifers, this tree loses its leaves with the branchlets in the fall. Fruit—a ball-shaped cone with thick scales, about 1 inch in diameter. Clues—odd-shaped "knees" that project above the mud-line around base of tree; broad buttresses flaring from trunk several feet above mud line. When this species grows on dry ground, neither the knees nor the buttresses develop. They obviously help stabilize the tree in the watery area.

This tree is a dominant species in the Cypress Slough ecosystem and appears elsewhere in the Big Thicket region.

Swamp Tupelo
Nyssa aquatica

Preferred habitat: swamps
Also called: swamp gum
Height—to 100 feet. Bark—dark brown, with vertical furrows roughened by small scales. Leaves—5–10 inches long, 2–4 inches wide; alternate, egg-shaped and tapering to a point; dark green and shiny above, pale and downy beneath. Fruit—about 1 inch long; purple; oblong; tough-skinned; acrid to the taste. Clues—conspicuous buttress flares from trunk above base to support the tree in its swampy site.

This tree is closely akin to the black tupelo, also called black gum, *Nyssa sylvatica,* which occupies dry ground and lacks the noticeable buttress. Its leaves are among the first in late summer or early fall to turn red and purple.

Swamp tupelo is a dominant species in the Cypress Slough ecosystem and appears in swamps throughout the Big Thicket region.

Basket Oak
Quercus michauxii

Preferred habitat: stream bottomlands
Also called: swamp chestnut oak, cow oak
Height—to 100 feet. Bark—light gray on older trees; divided into strips or flakes. Leaves—4–8 inches long; downy below; oblong-ovate in shape with distinctive wavy margins due to rounded lobes; sometimes turning crimson in fall. Fruit—acorn about 1½ inch long; shiny brown; set in shallow cup. "Sweet" compared with most acorns and gobbled up by wildlife, even eaten by cows. Basket weavers use the wood for strips.

Dominant Trees

Basket oak is a dominant species in the Palmetto-Hardwood and Oak-Gum Floodplain ecosystems. It occurs in other locations in the Big Thicket region.

Laurel Oak
Quercus laurifolia

Preferred habitat: moist locations
Height—to 100 feet. Bark—dark brown, may be tinged with red; somewhat rough. Leaves—resemble willow leaves, but broader; semi-evergreen; oblong in shape, 2½–4 inches long and about 1 inch wide, tapering to point. Fruit—egg-shaped acorn about ½ inch long; dark brown or almost black. This tree is similar in appearance to the willow oak, *Quercus phellos,* but the leaf of laurel oak is slightly larger and is semi-evergreen. The leaf of the willow oak turns pale yellow in fall and separates from the twig.

This tree is a dominant species of the Palmetto-Hardwood ecosystem and occurs elsewhere in the Big Thicket region.

Overcup Oak
Quercus lyrata

Preferred habitat: moist bottomlands
Also called: swamp post oak
Height—to 70 feet. Bark—brownish gray, rough; sheds in sizable plates. Leaves—7–9 inches long, 1–4 inches broad; oblong, narrowed at base; dark green above, lighter below;

pointed lobes; often turn red in fall. Fruit—fat acorn, ½–1 inch long, almost covered by cup.

Overcup oak is a dominant species in the Palmetto-Hardwood and Oak-Gum Floodplain ecosystems. It occurs in other locations in the Big Thicket region.

Sweetgum
Liquidambar styraciflua

Preferred habitat: river and stream bottomlands; also uplands
Also called: red gum
Height—to 120 feet. Bark—light gray; roughened into furrows and some scales. Leaves—star-shaped; five to seven lobes; about 6 inches across; aromatic; gorgeously colored in fall, from light yellow to red, orange, bronze, and purple. Fruit—dry, horn-tipped seed balls; 1–1½ inches in diameter; often seen swinging on the bare trees in winter. Clues—corky "wings" on the bark of twigs; star-shaped leaves; brilliant fall hues; distinctive seed balls.

This tree is a dominant species in the Oak-Gum Floodplain ecosystem and occurs plentifully in other Big Thicket areas.

Willow Oak
Quercus phellos

Preferred habitat: lowlands, borders of streams, rich, sandy uplands
Also called: pin oak (not the well-known pin oak of the Appalachian and North Central states, *Quercus palustris.*)
Height—to 110 feet. Bark—reddish brown, often streaked with whitish marks; relatively smooth; as tree ages, the bark becomes rougher. Leaves—2–5 inches long, ½–1 inch wide; resembling in shape the leaves of the black willow; light green and shiny above, dull below; alternate on twig. Fruit—acorn about ½ inch long in shallow cup.

This tree is a dominant species in the Oak-Gum Floodplain ecosystem and occurs randomly in the Big Thicket region.

Water Oak
Quercus nigra

Preferred habitat: rich bottomlands, borders of swamps
Height—to 80 feet. Bark—smooth; light brown to black-ish, often tinged with red; numerous thin scales on trunk. Leaves—variable in shape, but mostly oblong and broader near the point; dull, bluish green above, paler below; 2–3 inches long, ½ inch wide; turn yellow in fall. Fruit—acorn ½–⅔ inch long; often striped, light brown; cup covers only the base.

This tree is a dominant species in the Oak-Gum Flood-plain ecosystem and occurs abundantly in the Big Thicket region.

River Birch
Betula nigra

Preferred habitat: rich soils on borders of water courses
Also called: red birch
Height—to 60 feet. Bark—peels back in distinctive cinna-mon-colored or brownish layers. Leaves—2–3 inches long; oval with wedge-shaped base, double-toothed edge; dark green above, yellowish green below. Fruit—a cone-shaped bur about 1 inch long, densely packed with winged nutlets. Clue—the curling, shaggy bark.

This tree is a dominant species in the River Edge eco-system and occurs frequently on stream borders in the Big Thicket region.

Black Willow
Salix nigra

Preferred habitat: edges of streams, rivers
Height—to 50 feet. Bark—light brown to nearly black; rough and shaggy on old trees; deeply divided into ridges and plates. In winter, the naked twigs take on a golden or pinkish hue. Leaves —less than ½ inch wide, 3–6 inches long; tapered; bright green on both sides, turning yellow in fall. Fruit—a capsule, ¼ inch long, containing small seeds attached to long hairs, the hairs aiding in wind-borne distribution. Clue—the narrow, graceful leaves that inspired the term "willowy"; the coloring of winter twigs.

This tree is a dominant species in the River Edge eco-system and grows abundantly in the Big Thicket region.

American Sycamore
Platanus occidentalis

Preferred habitat: near streams, bottomlands
Also called: buttonwood, plane-tree
Height—to 170 feet. Considered the largest hardwood tree in North America. Bark—greenish gray, smooth, flaking off in patches to reveal white younger bark underneath and thereby creating striking abstract patterns on the trunk. Bark on older trees darkens into brown and divides into deep furrows around base. Leaves—4–9 inches long and about as broad; often coarsely toothed on margins; rather leathery; usually three to five lobes; bright green above, paler below; simple and alternate on stem. Fruit—a ball about 1 inch in diameter, composed of densely packed one-seeded nutlets.

Sycamore is a dominant species in the River Edge eco-system and occurs randomly in the Big Thicket region.

Whatever trail you walk or paddle in the Big Thicket, you'll see and hear birds. On land and water your companions will be birds of many sizes, markings, and voices; from ground feeders to tree-trunk pounders, from shoreline waders to high-sky acrobats soaring on the air currents.

It's no wonder that birding has become one of the most popular pastimes of Big Thicket visitors and residents. Booted and binoculared, they can be found virtually every weekend of the year seeking new sightings in the Thicket's extraordinary range of bird habitats.

The official habitats include: mixed evergreen-hardwood forests, grasslands, marshes, open fields with scattered trees and farmland, upland pine forests, river and creek shorelines, thickets, and open water. The latter habitat embraces oxbow ponds, swamps, rivers, and reservoirs. Such diversity provides a veritable smorgasbord of foods and protective cover preferred by hundreds of species of birds.

The conservative National Park Service shows 178 species of Big Thicket birds on its latest checklist, compiled in 1988. That's a remarkable roster for so small a geographical area as the Big Thicket. Even so, it doesn't tell the whole story.

Situated between America's two great flyways, the central and the Mississippi, the Big Thicket attracts numbers of well-known and yet unlisted migrants. Roger Tory Peterson, the nation's most celebrated authority on birds and birding, notes in his classic, *A Field Guide to the Birds of Texas,* that more than 540 species are recorded in the Long Star State—"the No. 1 Bird State," he writes—and the total may well exceed 800 if subspecies are counted.

Of course not all of these kinds of birds visit or reside in the Big Thicket. But the Thicket's nearness to the great migratory flyways, plus its unexcelled diversity of habitats, heightens a birder's chances for discovering the unexpected.

Veteran birders know, too, that the Big Thicket National Preserve covers only a small portion of the entire Big Thicket region. Records of sightings inside the boundaries will not include all bird species visiting the region.

One birder in the Tyler County community of Harmony, for example, swears that peregrine falcons are nesting near his acreage, which includes both woods and expanses of open fields. If true, their presence would be a shock, indeed. Peregrines haven't been authenticated in the area for decades. "Extirpated east of Rockies by pesticides," Peterson notes in his 1980 work, *Eastern Birds.* "Rare migrant, mainly along coast," he says of the species. But the Tyler County birder, living about one hundred miles from the coast of the Gulf of Mexico, is a retired Air Force fighter pilot who claims he recognizes the fantastic predatory speed and behavior of the peregrine falcon, a speed almost unmatched in birddom. His friends await an ornithologist's confirmation of the presence.

The legendary bird of the Big Thicket is the ivory-billed woodpecker, a gigantic creature nearly two feet long with a flaming scarlet crest and dramatic black-and-white body markings. Alas, the ivory-billed is believed to be long gone from the United States, where the Big Thicket was one of its last habitats, if not the very last. For years the species was thought to be extinct, a victim of demolished virgin forests, its sole habitat. However, a nesting pair of a related species was discovered several years ago in Cuba, so the ivory-billed may not have disappeared from the earth altogether.

New birders in the Big Thicket often believe they've spotted an ivory-billed when they see the pileated woodpecker, which bears similarities. The pileated is almost as large as the ivory-billed and its coloration is generally the same: bright red crest, black-and-white body markings.

But seasoned birders know the tell-tale signs of the ivory-billed: large white wing patches when the bird is resting (not sizable at all on the pileated) . . . the trailing white edge of the wing in flight (on the pileated, there's a white front edging) . . . and a half-dozen other physical and behavioral traits, including a white bill.

"But look! that big woodpecker's bill is white!" exclaims a first-time sighter of the pileated in the Big Thicket. Sunshine glinting off the bird's bill whitens it momentarily. Then the sun shifts and the gleam disappears, revealing the black bill of the pileated.

A sight in its own right, the pileated grows to almost twenty inches in length. In the Thicket old-timers know it as the "Godamighty bird." A view of the huge bird pounding a tree trunk for its dinner, the sound of which can easily carry for a mile, often produces the exclamation, "Godamighty, look at that woodpecker!"

Birding

Today, the rarest bird in the Big Thicket is another woodpecker, the red-cockaded. In 1970 it was declared an endangered species.

Medium-sized, the red-cockaded matures at about eight-and-a-half inches long and lives in the cavities of old trees of mixed pine-hardwood forests. A clan of red-cockadeds will number from two to nine birds. They prefer trees infested by red-heart fungus, which rots the heartwood and makes an easier job of chipping out cavities for nests. These white-cheeked birds were once plentiful in the Big Thicket, but commercial logging has virtually wiped out their habitat and threatened the survival of the species.

Big Thicket birders use a standard five-notch scale to indicate the frequency of recorded species: Abundant, Common, Uncommon, Occasional, and Rare. Seasons for recording sightings are divided thus: spring, March through May; summer, June through August; fall, September through November; winter, December through February.

Because new birders find it easier to identify species while exploring certain habitats, the checklist in Appendix A is organized by habitat headings. Every trail-trekker knows, of course, that all natural creatures and plants have a way of confounding the norms. A comprehensive field guide with full-color illustrations, such as Peterson's *Eastern Birds,* is indispensable for identifying the various species.

Bare essentials of birding in the Big Thicket include high-quality binoculars, pencil and notepad, comfortable walking shoes or boots, fair to excellent hearing, curiosity, patience, tolerance for the raw enthusiasms and errors of novices, and a willingness to be walking a trail at dawn, hearkening to the songs of male birds declaring their territories. (Female birds don't sing.)

The rewards of Big Thicket birding include seeing beauty and grace as if for the first time every time, and the companionship of people of all ages noted for their observational skills, knowledge, and unfailing good humor. Bird-watchers and carnivorous plant-watchers often cross paths in the Thicket's moist clearings, where tasty small bugs abound for the appetites of birds and plants alike.

Some Special Plants

How Carnivorous Plants Dine

Most visitors to the Big Thicket want to see the carnivorous plants at table. The best time to watch the process is late spring, after newly born bugs are out and about. You'll easily find pitcher-plants and sundews in their usual habitats, such as the Sundew Trail and the Pitcher Plant Trail. More difficult to find are the butterworts, but it's possible. And if any reader figures out an easy way to watch a bladderwort snare and snack on its prey, the author will cook him or her an iron pot full of red bean–sausage–chicken gumbo and a Cajun fig-pecan pie for dessert.

The finest photographs ever shot of the carnivorous plants of the Big Thicket appear in the March, 1993, issue of *Texas Highways* magazine. They're the work of an artist with camera, Joe Liggio. Maybe you can find a copy of that issue and take it to the field to help in identification of the various butterworts and bladderworts.

The pitcher-plant, which is no problem to identify, lures an insect to the mouth of its tube by a perfume released from the collar under the hood. The prey descends the tube looking for sweet eats. When it tries to backtrack up the tube, down-curving hairs resist. Some insects can't overcome this resistance and fall into the juice at the bottom of the tube, where their flesh is dissolved. When the meat's all gone, pitcher-plants leave the "bones" and tough parts of the insect. If you take a dead stalk from a brown pitcher-plant and slit the bottom with your knife, the bones of last year's dinners will tumble out. Some scientists figure that the pitcher-plant—and this is also presumed true of the other carnivorous plants—wants the nitrogen of insect flesh.

Sundews and butterworts operate alike. Their leaves lie flat on the ground exuding nectar that attracts insects. Take an ant, for example. Its feet get stuck in the nectar.

With its prey thus trapped, the plant signals its leaves to start digesting the ant's flesh. If the ant struggles, the chemistry of the plant responds by increasing the flow of digestive juices. The same fate awaits gnats, small flies, and other bugs that can't unstick their feet from the deadly goo.

Bladderworts are sinister and fantastic in their methods. The plant rises on pontoons above the surface of the pond. Its traps dangle below, closed chambers swishing in the little currents or stirrings. A water bug comes swimming by. It touches a trap's hair trigger, which springs open a door to a chamber. Water rushes into the chamber, carrying the bug with it. The door shuts, barring escape. Then the digestive juices go to work.

Of North America's five groups of carnivorous plants, four are indigenous to the Big Thicket. Only the Venus flytrap of the Carolinas is missing, and some prankster has mail-ordered and planted one of those.

Lichens

Lichen lovers will be glad to know that research has finally begun on tallying the Big Thicket species of this symbiotic marriage of primitive life forms. A lichen is a complex of algae and fungi growing together in mutual sustenance on a solid surface, such as a rock or tree trunk. They make lovely colors and patterns together.

To date, different kinds of lichens have been identified in ten units of the National Preserve, as follows: Lance Rosier Unit, 37 species; Loblolly Unit, 16; Menard Creek Corridor Unit, 19; Big Sandy Creek Unit, 24; Beech Creek Unit, 17; Turkey Creek Unit, 12; Jack Gore Baygall Unit, 16; Upper Neches River Corridor, 5; Lower Neches River, 20; Beaumont Unit, 7.

A Note about Mushrooms

Field and laboratory work proceeds at a scientific pace—you know how speedy that can be—on the enormous realm of mushrooms in the Big Thicket.

"Thousands," says David Lewis, the ranking authority, when asked about how many species of mushrooms live in the Thicket. His own herbarium holds about a thousand specimens. Much of his work has been displayed in northern museums.

If mushrooms fascinate you, as they do a lot of nature lovers, write to Lewis, c/o Texas Myecological Society, 455 Virginia Lane, Vidor, TX 77662. His phone number is (409) 769-3990. The society arranges several field trips each year.

Meantime, get your hands on a book, *Texas Mushrooms,* by Susan and Van Metzler. It presents fabulous photographs by Joe Liggio and other photographers that help in identifying major species. They make you shake your head in wonder at the beauty and diversity of plant life in the Big Thicket. That wonder extends to critters as well.

7 Critters of the Thicket

Most Big Thicket critters will hide from you, and some venture out only at night or in the twilight hours. But with forethought and a piece of luck, you can watch many of them and enjoy their ways.

Scientific records say more than fifty species of mammals live here, along with thirty kinds of amphibians, ninety-eight kinds of fishes, and sixty varieties of reptiles. Of that latter group, you'll want to give six a howdy-do and wide berth—the alligator, the southern copperhead, western cottonmouth, canebrake rattlesnake, pygmy rattlesnake, and Texas coral snake.

However, I must point out that in decades of poking around these woods and waters, I haven't seen more than a dozen snakes all told, and only two of those were poisonous. Snakes are known to be warier of you than you are of them. After all, you're sixty to seventy times taller than they are. How would you react to an intruder about 360 feet tall? But a mean or mother alligator might show aggravation at your presence.

This chapter on critters won't deal with insects or birds. Birds rate their own chapter, and no tally of regional insect species has been undertaken or published, to my knowledge. We'll also skip the microscopic creatures, even while recognizing that in the long run they're likely to be more important in the scheme of life than big animals.

Mammals

Mammals are animals that produce milk, suckle their young, and grow hair.

The **Virginia opossum,** a plentiful resident of the Thicket, is a member of the oldest, most primitive group of mammals in the New World—the order of Marsupials. They haven't changed noticeably for at least fifty million years. Their most familiar distinction is the pouch developed by the female on her abdomen during the breeding season. In campfire or barbershop conversations you might hear that the female opossum is impregnated through the nostrils. That's a bit of folklore, and not so. When she gives birth to a litter, the young crawl into the pouch. Each baby, weighing about three grains or about eight to a teaspoon, attaches itself to a teat and holds on for about seven weeks. Favorite nesting sites of opossums include hollow trees, woodpiles, under buildings, and in underground burrows. The author found one in the bottom drawer of a bedroom chest; it had entered through a hole in the backing. Opossums come out at night to feed on rats, mice, insects, crustaceans, frogs, fruits, vegetables, and other such victuals.

Two **shrews**—the southern shorttailed shrew and least shrew—and the **eastern mole** represent the order of Insectivores (insect-eaters) in the Thicket. The mole has crude ways. It's not unusual for one of these animals to consume more than two-thirds of its body weight in eighteen hours, if enough earthworms, June-beetle larvae, and moth larvae can be found. It kills live prey by crushing the body against the side of its burrow, or piling loose earth on the prey and biting it.

Ten kinds of **bats** live in the Thicket or migrate in and out. Three species are common, (the red bat, Seminole bat, and evening bat), three are uncommon (the eastern pipistrelle, big brown, and southeastern myotis), two are migrants (silver-haired and hoary), and two more are considered possible visitors (northern yellow, and Rafinesque's big-eared bat). A bat of another family, the Brazilian free-tailed, is also believed by bat experts to visit the Thicket. These flying mammals with phenomenal hearing feed on insects and are considered highly beneficial.

That weird character of Texas lore, the **armadillo,** digs and waddles all over the Thicket. A native of South America, the nine-banded armadillo prefers to be near water where it can take mud baths. Armadillos are known to walk across the bottom of narrow streams or creeks, emerging on the other side. They don't require watery sites, however; they'll dig dens in manicured backyards. In sandy soil, a den might descend four feet and extend for a dozen to fifteen feet underground. Armadillos eat a tremendous variety of foods, from termites to reptiles. More than 90 percent of their food is animal matter. Although they may sample some garden vegetables, too, they're usually far more beneficial than harmful because of insect varmints they control.

Eastern cottontail, swamp rabbit, and black-tailed jack rabbit make up the **rabbit** population in the Thicket, with the first two counted as commonplace. The swamp rabbit weighs up to six pounds, twice as large as the cottontail, and grows dense fur. It swims rivers and streams easily, a trait not found in other Texas rabbits.

Three species of **squirrels** race and squawk through Thicket trees—the gray, fox, and southern flying squirrels. The flying squirrel doesn't actually fly, but rather glides from a higher limb to a lower one.

The only **gopher** in the Thicket is the plains pocket gopher, a small (quarter-pound to half-pound) digger whose underground tunnels meander through areas where it feeds. Students of gopher ways say a good place to look for them is under oak trees that have dropped an abundant crop of acorns.

Yes, the Thicket contains **beavers**, not in abundance, but they're here and making a comeback in numbers. They're hefty animals, weighing around forty pounds on the average.

Beavers need a pond, lake, river, or stream to prosper. They prefer small bodies of water near stands of willow. The inner bark of willows and other trees form a mainstay of their diet, although they feed on other vegetation as well. Their reputation for know-how in building dams to control water flow and burrows with "plunge-holes" comes well-earned. A typical beaver colony may have six or seven animals. Look for signs of beaver—gnawed sapling stumps, dams constructed of branches—in the Big Sandy Creek and Turkey Creek Units of the Big Thicket National Preserve. (See those sections of this Guide.)

Two other Thicket members of the order of Rodents that hold special interest are the muskrat and nutria. The muskrat ranks as a rare animal here and the nutria as uncommon.

Muskrats like marshes—shallow-water spots with clumps of cattails framed by bulrushes, sedges, and other wetland vegetation. They build domed lodges of marshy plants, about two feet in diameter at water level and sticking up maybe eighteen inches above water. A submerged plunge-hole provides access. If you find such a lodge, you'll likely also find travelways radiating outward to feeding areas. A muskrat family living on a stream or river, where a lodge wouldn't be practical, burrows a habitation with a submerged entrance out of the bank.

Hawks, owls, raccoons, foxes, minks, and large turtles prey upon muskrats. But probably the major predator is the human consortium of trapper–marketer–fur wearer, the developer who drains wetlands, and a society that pollutes waterways.

Nutrias, natives of South America, compete for habitat in the Big Thicket and elsewhere in the United States with the American muskrat and waterfowl. They were imported and established as a supposed "cure" for ponds and lakes choked with vegetation. The cure didn't work. They multiplied too rapidly for the available food supply where they had been stocked, and then moved into areas where they usurped the environs of native animals. In the Thicket, you might find their nests built of reeds and sedges near water.

Meat-eating animals of the Big Thicket, representatives of the order of Carnivores, include three species of canines, two of raccoons, five of weasels, one cat, and one deer.

This order once featured the black bear, jaguar, mountain lion, ocelot, and red wolf. All those dramatic animals have been shot out in the Big Thicket. The scientific term is exterminated.

More funny, winsome, and cuss-punctuated stories have been told about the "masked bandit" of the animal world than any other critter. One **raccoon** built its nest in a nail keg; another left its den and came to the screen door of the house when the owner of the farm put on Beethoven records; another made a daytime bed from a crow's nest twenty feet up a tree; many raid corn patches and up-end garbage cans carefully closed by farmers and campers. That's where the cussing comes in.

In the Thicket, raccoons may weigh up to thirty pounds, though that's big. They prefer to be near water, where they do most of their nightly foraging. They sleep during the day in dens usually found in hollow trees or logs. They enjoy nature's buffet—most everything from larvae wasps to grapes and persimmons to garden crops. Their favorite Thicket fare combines acorns and crawdads.

Two species of the raccoon family occupy the Thicket: the common raccoon and the rare ringtail. Both have alternating black and buff or white rings on the tail. The **ringtail** is much smaller, tipping in at two or three pounds, and resembles a fox except for its notably ringed tail. One reason the ringtail shows up rarely in the Thicket is that it prefers rocky sites. Plenty of rocky sites dot the upper Thicket—say, north of U.S. 190—but they're not as typical as woody sites. Ringtails are nocturnal roamers.

Another family of carnivores, **weasels** and their relatives, have five representatives in the Thicket—mink, river otter, striped skunk, eastern spotted skunk, and the long-tailed weasel. Of those members, only the striped skunk is commonly seen. A former resident of the Thicket, the hog-nosed skunk, has been exterminated. The eastern spotted skunk is only a possible inhabitant, and the mink and river otter are listed as uncommon. The long-tailed weasel is rare.

"Vicious and aggressive when cornered, a bundle of fury in the hand," is how one scientist, Dr. W. B. Davis, author of *The Mammals of Texas*, describes the personality of the **long-tailed weasel**. They're excellent climbers and swimmers, having no fear of swift waters. They prey on small rodents; pocket gophers constitute fine fare for them. They're noted for their curiosity about humans, peering out of one hole until discovered, then ducking out of sight and sticking their small heads out of another hole to keep watch.

Minks are colored dark chocolate brown with paler underparts. The animal has a small head and long neck and tail. Valued for its fur, the mink weighs up to three pounds. It's found near water, preferring small streams choked here and there by debris that provides concealment. They take over the dens of muskrats or may make a dwelling under tree roots, in a stream bank, or in a pile of branches and debris. They kill and eat ground squirrels, muskrats, rats, mice, fish, frogs, snakes, and birds, among other critters.

What creature could be more delightful than a **river otter** at play? Most good zoos keep river otters to wow onlookers at their water-slicked slides, and they've starred in a score of entertaining movies and film shorts. In the wild, they're difficult to find and observe, usually being very shy about strangers. (But see James Overstreet's experience in "Trail Notes.")

Lakes and larger waterways provide habitat for river otters. They may cover miles in the search for fish and crawdads to satisfy their appetites. A clay "slide" on a stream bank offers recreation, or so it seems when they stop to play "follow the leader," legs folded under their bodies as they whiz into the water.

Their dens might be hollow logs, hollow trees, or tree roots at the edge of water. A pair of river otters may mate for life, and both parents take care of the offspring.

Of the cat family, only the **bobcat** remains in the Thicket, and its numbers are dwindling.

Shallow nitwits who wear fur to impress other nitwits have played upon the greed of bobcat trappers. And some hunters can't resist shooting a bobcat any time it fails to hide itself completely. A couple of years ago, in Woodville, two hunters drove slowly all over town with the body of a bobcat, a superb specimen, lashed across the hood of their pickup truck. It's the only time I have seen a vehicle driven in such a way as to be prancing—kind of jerking and creeping. Oh, to be admired for such prowess with a high-powered weapon!

Very shy creatures, bobcats make their dens in thickets and climb trees to take refuge from hunting dogs. They begin seeking food before nightfall and continue the search during the dark hours. Mice, rats, ground squirrels, and rabbits are favorite foods. About half their diet consists of animals harmful to human habitations, such as mice and rats. A springtime litter contains two to seven young, beautifully spotted and furred. The kittens stay close to their mother until fall, when they show capabilities for handling their own needs. The color of their adult fur combines reddish brown or gray tones streaked with black, and white underparts with black spots. They usually grow to a weight of twelve to thirty pounds, sometimes more.

Three magnificent species of cats are no longer found in the Big Thicket: jaguar, mountain lion, and ocelot. The largest carnivore of Thicket legend, the black bear, is also missing. All of these dramatic species have been shot-out or trapped-out.

Still on the "live" lists are the gray fox, red fox, and coyote, but only the gray fox is listed as common in the Thicket.

The remaining mammal of the Big Thicket is the most popular big game animal in Texas, the **white-tailed deer.** Adult weight can vary from sixty to around two hundred pounds. You can often observe small groups of white-tails feeding in open fields near woods soon after sunrise and shortly before sunset. Vegetarians, they like grasses, the leaves and twigs of wild shrubs, fruits, acorns, and a wide variety of other plant foods. A white-tailed deer may stay close to one territory for years, depending on the availability of forage and cover.

Trophy-seekers sometimes guess a deer's age by the points of its antlers, but they're only fooling themselves. In its first year, a fawn will grow a set of spike antlers, but afterwards the points have no correlation with age. The diameter of the beam of the antlers offers a better clue: the thicker the older—usually, but not always. The animal's lifelong nutrition may well determine the development of its antlers.

Its teeth provide a better way to gauge a deer's age. Permanent teeth replace all "milk teeth" at the age of two years. But after that, it's a matter of wear and tear from grinding food, and age becomes a question mark.

The mother hides newborn fawns in brush. She nurses them several times each day for about two weeks, until they have strength enough to move about with her and learn the ways of animals hunted by humans with weapons of space-age technology.

Amphibians

Amphibians are animals with backbones that adapt to life on both land and water. Their group includes frogs, toads, newts, salamanders, and some tropical species that look like worms.

Salamanders are often confused with lizards, but a thin, smooth, moist skin identifies a salamander quickly. Lizards have skins made up of scales or plates. Salamanders, being amphibians, stay closer to water than lizards. Scientists also count differences in toes on the front feet to be sure—four for salamanders, five for lizards. Picky, eh? Besides, lizards are reptiles, not amphibians.

The dwarf salamander is the only species believed to be common in the Big Thicket National Preserve. Three others—the marbled salamander, eastern tiger salamander, and central newt— are listed as uncommon but present.

Scientists show six more salamanders as being documented in the region. They are: western lesser siren, spotted salamander, mole salamander, three-toed amphiuma, southern dusky salamander, and Gulf Coast water dog. Experts suspect that the smallmouthed salamander lives in or around the Thicket because the conditions are right, but its presence hasn't been documented.

Frogs

Nineteen species of **frogs** and **toads** reside around here, but perhaps not for long. As this text is being written, scientists throughout the world are expressing alarm at the rapidly decreasing numbers of frogs. If that sounds like much ado about a small, ugly critter, look to the reason for the alarm—a world environment lethal to even one species of plant or animal becomes threatening to all. All living creatures depend on several basic elements for life, health, and continuity.

The transformation from a water-borne "pollywog"—a long-tailed larvae with gills—into a terrestrial frog or toad with lungs, is one of nature's magical tricks.

In the **treefrog** family, six species are commonly found in the Thicket: northern cricket frog, gray treefrog, green treefrog, northern spring peeper, squirrel treefrog, and upland chorus frog. Two members of the treefrog family—the coastal cricket frog and Strecker's chorus frog—probably occur here but just haven't been found by a documenting scientist.

In the **true frog** family, the bullfrog, bronze frog, and southern leopard frog are common. The southern crawfish frog is uncommon, and the pig frog and pickerel frog are only probable.

Toads

How to tell a toad from a frog? **Toads** usually have warty skins, frogs smooth skin. Toads are often found far from water in dry habitats; frogs usually stay near water. Toads have fatter bodies than frogs and move rather sluggishly, hence the term toady.

The East Texas toad, Gulf Coast toad, and eastern narrowmouth toad are common Thicket residents. Uncommonly found is Hurter's spadefoot toad. The Great Plains narrowmouth toad is thought to be here but isn't yet documented.

Reptiles

Reptiles range from lizards to alligators, with turtles and snakes for kin. They're all cold-blooded animals, meaning their blood temperature changes with the heat or cold of their surroundings. Birds and mammals, on the other hand, maintain an internal temperature despite outside conditions, except in extremes. No other single trait distinguishes reptiles from all other creatures, as feathers distinguish birds, but most reptiles share common characteristics. Their skin is usually divided into scales or plates, they breathe with lungs instead of gills, and the ones with feet have five clawed toes on each foot. Most eat animals, but the land tortoise is an exception. Most lay eggs, the exception being the poisonous pit vipers, who give birth to live young. At one time, some reptiles flew like birds, but that was millions of years ago. Reptiles are an individualistic and varied bunch. They live in just about all temperate and tropical habitats, from deserts to freshwater floodplains to saltwater grasslands. The Thicket has its share of reptiles and then some.

Turtles

A **turtle** is a reptile with a shell on its back. The shields of the shell are called scutes. Turtles don't have teeth (they're the only reptiles so lacking), but their bite can still inflict a painful wound.

Fifteen species of turtles live here. The commoners include the snapping turtle, Mississippi mud turtle, three-toed box turtle, and red-eared slider. Uncommon members of this clan are the alligator snapping turtle, razorback musk turtle, Mississippi map turtle, Sabine map turtle, ornate box turtle, smooth softshell, and pallid spiny softshell.

Four more are probables: stinkpot turtle, Texas diamondback terrapin, western chicken turtle, and Metter's river cooter.

Lizards

"They say the Lion and Lizard keep the courts where Jamshyd gloried and drank deep." So wrote the poet Omar Khayyam about the lizard's liking for old ruins, be they castles or East Texas shanties. Jamshyd is not a rock star, as might be supposed from the description, but an ancient high-liver in Persian legend.

A definition of a **lizard** comes hard to biologists. Most agree it's a reptile with scales on its skin, ears, and eyelids. Lizards have four legs, except one of their kind, the glass lizard, which moves about without any legs.

Anyone who has tried to nab a lizard by the tail has been left holding a piece of the tail. Put the broken piece down right away and watch it wiggle. Lizards developed this trick in their evolution, hoping that the wiggle would confuse a hungry enemy while the previous owner escaped. A new tail, though shorter, will grow in place.

Of the ten lizard species in the Thicket, only three show themselves in common numbers: the green anole, five-lined skink, and ground skink. Three others are less commonly seen: the northern fence lizard, broadhead skink, and six-lined racerunner. Then appear three not yet documented in the Preserve but found elsewhere in the Thicket region: the Mediterranean gecko, western slender glass lizard, and Texas horned lizard. Finally, there's the southern coal skink, a definite but undocumented possibility.

Snakes

Snakes are amazing creatures that do far more good than harm, from a human perspective, and which occupy an essential niche in nature.

They live exclusively on animals: rats, mice, frogs, toads, salamanders, and the like. Hidden much of the time, they curl up in piles of leaves, logs, stumps, mounds of vegetation, collections of debris. They like the woods and edges of creeks, streams, and bogs.

When a snake flicks its tongue, it's sampling dust particles to get the taste and smell of the area. It has outstanding powers of sight and smell. It "hears" by its body, sensing vibrations from the ground. Several times a year, most snakes shed their skins, simply crawling out head first.

Snake-watchers like hot still nights after a rain. On such nights, insects emerge from their hideouts in great numbers. Toads and frogs appear in proportionate numbers to feed on the insects. Snakes appear to feast on frogs and toads. Snake-watchers appear with flashlights to study the whole process.

Most snakes let you have your way when your paths cross. When one doesn't, let it have its way. In the wild, watch where you put your hands and feet, so that you don't surprise a snake. Even nonpoisonous snakes can inflict a painful bite. In the event of a bite by a venomous snake, get to the nearest doctor or hospital without further ado. Most such bites are effectively treated early on. All need quick, professional attention. See the locations and phone numbers of Big Thicket area hospitals in Appendix E.

Nonpoisonous snakes of the Big Thicket—
common species:

Texas rat snake	eastern hognose snake
yellowbelly water snake	eastern rough green snake
Texas brown snake	western ribbon snake

Nonpoisonous—uncommon species:

eastern garter snake	Florida redbelly
Gulf crayfish snake	diamondback water snake
Gulf salt marsh snake	eastern coachwhip
speckled kingsnake	western mudsnake
corn snake	eastern yellowbelly racer
tan racer	buttermilk racer

Nonpoisonous species in Thicket counties, but not yet
documented in the National Preserve:

northern scarlet snake	Mississippi ringneck snake
prairie snake	Louisiana rough green snake
Louisiana pine snake	Graham's crawfish snake
marsh brown snake	flathead snake
Gulf Coast ribbon snake	rough earth snake

The western smooth green snake is another nonpoisonous
snake considered a probable resident.

Poisonous species: The southern copperhead and western cottonmouth are listed as common, and the following three as uncommon: Texas coral snake, canebrake rattlesnake, and western pygmy rattlesnake.

Alligators

Tyrone was his name, after the handsome heartthrob of the movies in the late 1930s and for some years thereafter, Tyrone Power. He acquired the name through the humor of the Alabama and Coushatta Indians, on whose reservation he lived. He was probably the ugliest alligator in Polk County, maybe in the entire Big Thicket.

Tyrone would lumber out of his mud bed beside a small creek when he heard the bus coming. The bus, an open-window vehicle driven by a member of the tribes, would be filled with tourists on a bumpy ramble through deep woods of the Big Thicket that cover part of the Indian reservation.

Tyrone, the alligator who met the tourist bus daily, perhaps to let folks snap his portrait.

A ten-foot-long monster out of a horror movie, Tyrone would find a spot near the dirt road of the bus's route, belly-down and wait. As the bus rounded a curve in the woods, the driver would suddenly announce, "And there's old Tyrone waiting for us to take his picture."

The driver would stop some yards away from the alligator, the riders with cameras would disembark, and Tyrone would pose, seeming to grin, as long as anybody wanted to take his picture. Sometimes, as the bus pulled away, you could see Tyrone turning around and heading back to his mud bed. Everybody on the bus sure was happy to have seen him.

Tyrone met the bus tour for years back in the late 1970s and early 1980s, but he hasn't been seen for a long time now. Maybe he died, or moved on during the drought years to a better, wetter spot.

Alligators live in several places in the Big Thicket. All are considered dangerous. Tyrone himself may have been waiting for a leg or an arm to get close enough to snap up, a possibility always announced by the Indian driver in warning his customers to stay a double-safe distance while Tyrone posed for their cameras.

Alligators are the most awesome reptiles of the Thicket, or almost anywhere else they're encountered in the American wild. The largest reptiles in North America, they grow to fifteen feet in length. The male's bellow during mating season makes a sound to remember.

"It doesn't attract females," writes one alligator expert,

"it's meant to intimidate other males." Actually, females can enter the bellower's territory at will. But if a male crosses the line, a monumental thrashing occurs.

When a female alligator mates and gets ready to lay her eggs, she builds a nest of debris and mud about three feet high and six feet in diameter. Then she makes a depression in the summit of the mound, and there deposits twenty to sixty eggs. She covers the eggs with more vegetation, then guards the nest fiercely for about ten weeks, until the eggs hatch. The young 'gators may follow her around for a year or so afterward. *Critters*

Alligators bask on the banks of waterways, in shallow water, at times on dry land. Fishes, small mammals, turtles, and birds make up an adult's diet. The young fatten on frogs and crustaceans.

In the Big Thicket wild alligators aren't easy to find, for which visitors and the 'gators themselves can both be thankful. In 1992, Lynn Barnes of Chester reported a twelve-foot 'gator lying across a dirt road outside the community. He almost ditched his pickup truck steering a wide berth around the animal. On the return trip a few hours later, the 'gator was gone. Their favorite habitats include remote swamps, river edges, freshwater courses, large ponds. A nearby place where they can be watched under wild but safer circumstances is from a marsh boat in Sea Rim Park, a few miles west of Port Arthur. It's not a Big Thicket locale, but not far distant.

Perhaps Tyrone left a showboat offspring that basks in a creek by a turn of the road on the Big Thicket Bus Tour of the Alabama-Coushatta Reservation.

That bus ride in the woods is just one of many recreational activities offered at the Indian Reservation and elsewhere in the Thicket.

8   Recreation and Attractions

Alabama-Coushatta Reservation

Legendary hero Sam Houston led a political fight to establish the Alabama-Coushatta Indian Reservation in 1854 as a reward for the Indians' role in the Texas War of Independence. Since then the reservation, located between Woodville and Livingston, has expanded to 4,181 acres and become a major tourist attraction not only in the Big Thicket but in the whole state of Texas.

Among the special events, facilities, and services offered at the reservation are:

Annual Pow-Wow, usually held the first week in June, when hundreds of Indians from various tribes around the United States come to the reservation to perform and palaver.

Open-air bus tours of the deep Big Thicket woods on the reservation.

Indian Country Tour, also aboard the open-air bus, with visits to Indian homes, hunting grounds, and campsites reminiscent of pioneer days.

Indian Chief Train Ride. Climb aboard a real train, mini-size, for a chug and whistle through the reservation and surrounding woods.

Tribal Dance Square. Indian dancers in colorful regalia perform to heady chants and drumbeats.

Living Indian Village and Historical Museum. Relics of earlier times, when the Alabama and Coushatta tribes emigrated to East Texas from Alabama in the late 1700s.

Inn of the Twelve Clans Restaurant. A full-service restaurant with banquet facilities.

Arts and Crafts Gift Shop. These tribes are justly famous for pine-needle baskets, marvelous in design and construction. The curing and weaving of the longleaf pine needles is becoming a lost Indian art. Weavers create their own designs, often in the shape of actual or native and mythical animals.

The Indian Chief Railroad delights passengers on its run through woods on the Alabama-Coushatta Reservation. (Reservation photo.)

Open-air bus ride combines Big Thicket wild scenery and history of Indian Reservation. (Reservation photo)

Complete camping facilities, including cabins, primitive sites, and RV stations with full hookups.

Lake Tombigbee. A twenty-six–acre lake stocked with fish. Lakeside facilities include camp sites, area lighting, picnic tables, fire rings, drinking water, a swimming area, and nature trails.

The campgrounds and a convenience store are open year-round, but other activities are seasonal. The convenience store offers gasoline, groceries, fishing supplies, and a washateria. The usual season extends from March through November. For information, write to Indian Reservation, Route 3 Box 640, Livingston, TX 77351. Phone (409) 563–4391.

Neches River Boat Ride

Take a leisurely look at the moody waters and mossy swamps of the Big Thicket aboard a ninety-minute Neches

The Eagle Dance performed by Indian youth in show at Alabama-Coushatta Reservation. (Reservation photo)

River boat ride operated by Timber Ridge Tours. The boat leaves at 1:00 P.M., 3:00 P.M., and 5:00 P.M. on Saturdays and Sundays, usually April through September, from a dock near Silsbee. No reservations. James Overstreet, the skipper, knows plenty of Big Thicket lore, which he expounds during the trip along the river and its sloughs. Call him or his wife, Nelda, at (409) 246–3107 for information, or write Timber Ridge Tours at P.O. Box 115, Kountze, TX 77625. Inquire about trailer hookups if you're interested in such.

Each pine-needle basket has a unique design and craftsmanship. Available at Gift Shop, Alabama-Coushatta Indian Reservation.

Pioneer Hamlet

Heritage Village, a mile west of Woodville, contains several pioneer-era buildings, including a superb hand-hewn log home, the Tolar Cabin, built in 1866, and a reconstructed 1860s general store. The simulated village also has a livery stable, church, barber shop, sheriff's office, blacksmith's shop, chair factory, schoolhouse, and a dozen or more other structures depicting early East Texas community life. Genuine artifacts enhance the character of each shop or office. The village features a working jeweler and an excellent Museum Store and Gift Shop. Admission fee charged. Next door is the Pickett House Restaurant, well known for its collection of circus posters and family-style meals. Contact: Heritage Village Museum, P.O. Box 888, Woodville, TX 75979. Phone: (409) 283–2272. Pickett House phone: (409) 283–3946.

Naturalist Programs for Children and Adults

Rangers of the Big Thicket National Preserve conduct more than twenty excellent programs on nature appreciation and outdoors skills. Phone Preserve headquarters or a

One of several structures of Thicket yesteryears at Heritage Village near Woodville.

ranger station for information and registration concerning the programs of your choice. (See Appendix E.)

General Interest Programs

Big Thicket Night Prowl. Ages eight and up. A guided walk of two to three hours discovering the ways of night-prowling animals of the Thicket. Bring your own flashlight. Maximum group, fifteen persons; minimum, six.

Canoe Cook's Lake. A tour of four to five hours of scenic Cook's Lake near Beaumont. Bring your own canoe or a rented canoe. Maximum, ten canoes; minimum, two canoes. Ages eight and up.

Farm to Forest Hike. A guided five-mile, six-hour hike revealing ecological transitions from the farmland to mature woods. Big Sandy Creek Unit. Wear comfortable shoes and bring lunch. Maximum group, twenty-five persons; minimum, six persons. Ages eight and older.

Insects for Lunch. A walk of one to two hours to meet and observe insect-eating plants. Maximum group, twenty-five persons; minimum, six persons. Ages five and older.

Kirby Nature Trail Hike. Highly recommended for first-time visitors to the Big Thicket. A walk of about one-and-a-half hours through four ecosystems. Stately woods.

Streamside Stroll. Bring a trailside supper for this leisurely three-mile afternoon saunter. Also, bring insect repellent and drinks. Group maximum, twenty-five persons; minimum, six. Ages eight and older.

Tales of the Big Thicket. A one-hour yarn-spinning about characters and the unending lore of the Big Thicket. Group maximum, fifteen persons; minimum, six persons. Ages eight and older.

Through the Looking Glass. This one's for small children, ages five to twelve. A two-hour walk featuring close-up views of nature in form and function. Magnificence magnified! Group maximum, twenty-five persons; minimum, six persons.

Turkey Creek Trek. Plan for a six-hour hike through a rich mix of ecosystems. Bring lunch and water. Group maximum, twenty-five persons; minimum, six persons. Ages eight and older.

Village Creek Float. Stretch out on an inner tube and trickle down a beautiful creek for four to six hours, pausing here and there on sandbars. Bring your own inner tube. Also, bring lunch in a waterproof container, and drinks. Group maximum, twenty tubers; minimum, ten. Ages eight and older.

Wildflower Walk. A two-hour walk among the wildflowers in season, with pointers on locating and identifying the beauties.

Wild Food Foray. Scores of Big Thicket plants have been used for food and medicine by generations of natives. Here's a short course in that fascinating folklore on a walk of two to three hours. Ages eight and older.

Canoe Class on Franklin Lake. Want to go canoeing but don't know how? Here's a session on basic ways and means, plus a practice trip among big cypresses on a backwater slough of the Neches River. Bring your own canoe or a rented one. Maximum group, ten canoes.

Map and Compass Reading. Folks still get lost occasionally in the woods and swamps of the Big Thicket. You'll learn how to always know where you are in this two-hour class on the basics. And you'll test your new knowledge in the bargain. Ages eight and older.

Kids' Day Out. An outing for youngsters six to twelve years of age to stimulate and fulfill their curiosity about nature. Maximum group, fifteen; minimum, six.

Kid's Wilderness Survival. Simple ways for children to learn how to act and survive if lost in the wilderness. But wait a minute—adults need these tricks, too. This two-hour session, maybe a few minutes longer, prepares people from age five up. Maximum group, twenty; minimum, six.

Nature Crafts. How to use various art forms to express your admiration of nature. For children and adults. Two to three hours.

Beginning Birder's Workshop. No quick fix this. Workshops meet once a week for four weeks and take field trips, too. Each class covers two hours. When you've completed it, you're prepared for a lifetime of outdoor fun, fascination, and detective work among our feathered friends.

Introduction to Nature Photography. How-to sessions on close-ups, lighting, and composition to stretch your photographic skills. Plan on four evening sessions, each two hours in length.

Attention: area schools. In addition to the above activities, rangers of the Big Thicket National Preserve also conduct programs for school classes of any grades, and prepare special programs for elementary school students from grades one through six.

Meanwhile, at Saratoga . . .

At Saratoga in the mid-1960s, old school buildings were converted into the Big Thicket Museum. Until the late 1970s, the modest museum served not only to display Big Thicket artifacts and specimens but also as a headquarters for the grass-roots citizens movement to Save the Big Thicket. Then, in controversy, the property passed from the leaders and forces of that movement to other groups. In 1992, a plan was afoot for the National Park Service to come into possession of the property for development into an information station and exhibit hall for the traveling public. If the plan comes to pass, it would make ideal use of the location, a historic gateway to the largest unit in the Big Thicket National Preserve, the Lance Rosier Unit.

Any doubt why *Carpinus caroliniana* is sometimes called the muscle-tree?

Camping

Campers find a broad range of sites in the Big Thicket region, from rather luxurious facilities at the Chain-O-Lakes near Romayor to strictly primitive spots in several units of the Big Thicket National Preserve.

Developed Campgrounds Near the National Preserve

The following campgrounds were open and operating just prior to publication of this *Guide*. When you decide to go camping, call first. There may be additional or fewer campgrounds than this list indicates.

Alabama-Coushatta Indian Reservation. Located between Livingston and Woodville off U.S. 190; seventeen miles east of Livingston, then two miles south. Varying fees for tent sites with water and electricity, and full hookup sites. Open all year. Special tours and programs available in the summer season. Information: (409) 563–4391.

Chain-O-Lakes Campground and Resort. Located one mile southwest of Romayor off FM 787; take Daniel's Plantation Ranch Road. Contains 271 acres with 260 campsites. Varying fees for wilderness sites (without water or electricity), sites with full hookups, and water and electricity hookups. Picnic grounds available by day or per person per week. Semi-luxury cabins available. Reservations recommended. Call (713) 592–2150 for rates.

Woodsy Hollow Campground. 1.9 miles east of U.S. 59 on FM 2665. Full camping and recreational facilities. Pull-through sites with 30 amps. Call for rates. Belle or Virgil Jordan. (409) 365–3100.

Triple D Guest Ranch. Located outside the west boundary of Turkey Creek Unit of the Big Thicket National Preserve. Twelve cabins and rooms with air conditioning and electric heat; a bunkhouse with seventeen bunks. Most cabins have two double beds and two sets of bunks. Family-style eating. Bed and breakfast also available. Call or write for rates and reservations: Route 2, Box 458, Warren, TX 77664. (409) 547- 2248.

Big Thicket Campground. This new campground was under development at press time and provided only primi-

tive camping at that time. Located one-quarter mile off
FM 420, one-half mile east of U.S. 69. (Entrance next to
Providence Church). Primitive sites, water, pit toilet. Call
Craig Davis, proprietor: (409) 246–4817.

Oak Leaf Park. Full-service KOA campground located
at 6900 Oak Leaf Drive, Orange, TX 77630. Interstate 10
Eastbound from Beaumont, exit at 874-A just east of Texas
62. All hookups, modern showers and restrooms, store,
pool, laundry, recreation hall, fishing, cabins, and restaurant. RV's lower fees. Call for rates (409) 886–4082.

Big Thicket Outpost and Campground. A small fifteen-site wooded campground with full hookups for RV's.
Varying fees for sites with water. Showerhouse, picnic tables, and grills available also. Located on U.S. 69/287 one
mile north of FM 420, just south of Village Mills. Call
(409) 246–2433.

Lake Tejas. "Best swimmin' hole in East Texas," says the
Colmesneil Independent School District, which owns this
facility, developed in the late 1930s during the Great
Depression. Open for the summer season. Besides a large
protected area for swimmers, Lake Tejas offers fishing,
camping, hook-ups for RV's, and shelters for family reunions or group meetings. One mile east of Colmesneil on
State Highway 256. Call (409) 837–9290 for fee schedules
and reservations.

Backcountry Camping in the National Preserve

Campers who like primitive conditions have a choice of
back-country camping zones in the following units of the
National Preserve:

Jack Gore Baygall Unit	Neches Bottom Unit
Big Sandy Creek Unit	Lance Rosier Unit
Beaumont Unit	Beech Creek Unit
Loblolly Unit	Turkey Creek Unit

Visual and noise separation must be maintained between
camped groups.

For those using the Neches River, camping is allowed
on sandbars, except at Lakeview Sandbar and other posted

day-use areas, or unless otherwise restricted in the regulations. During hunting season, from October 1 through January 15, all portions of the Beaumont, Beech Creek, Big Sandy Creek, Jack Gore Baygall, Neches Bottom, and Lance Rosier Units are closed to camping. A portion of Turkey Creek Unit is open year-round for camping.

A free backcountry permit is required and *must* be obtained prior to camping from any park ranger or at three locations (either in person or by telephone): (1) the Information Station on FM 420 in the Turkey Creek Unit—open daily from 9:00 A.M. to 5:00 P.M.; (2) Preserve headquarters in Beaumont at 3785 Milam—open weekdays between 8:00 A.M. and 4:30 P.M.; (3) the North District Ranger Office in Woodville on U.S. 287. Maps showing the specific zone locations are provided with the permit.

Camp safely! Take into account outdoor conditions. Bring insect repellent. Beware of poisonous snakes, poison ivy, and fire ants. Open water is not potable; bring drinking water. Do not rest or camp beneath dead or dying trees. Carry a first aid kit, map, and compass.

Campers' Bonanza

At Dam B and on Steinhagen Lake, extensive facilities concentrated in nine large parks on or near the Neches River welcome families, campers, fishers, and other outdoors enthusiasts.

Three of the sites located in Martin Dies, Jr. State Park are operated by Texas Parks and Wildlife, six by the U.S. Corps of Engineers.

Martin Dies, Jr. State Park. Martin Dies, Jr. State Park covers 705 lush acres with three units: Hen House, Walnut Ridge, and Cherokee. All three have electrical outlets for RVs, boat-launching ramps, drinking water, sanitary facilities, picnicking, camping areas, and trailer areas. In addition, the Hen House and Walnut Ridge Units also offer rental cabins, showers, nature trails, and fishing piers. The Walnut Ridge Unit has a large group facility for day use. Hen House Unit marks off a nice spot for river swimming. For information on fees and reservations, call (409) 384–5231.

What's better than a river swim on a summer afternoon? At Martin Dies, Jr. State Park.

The U.S. Corps of Engineers operates East End Park, Bluff View Park, Campers' Cove Park, Magnolia Ridge Park, Beech Grove Park, and Sandy Creek Park on the lake. All have drinking water and sanitary facilities. All except Bluff View Park have camping and trailer areas. Other facilities vary from park to park. For more information, write or call U.S. Corps of Engineers, Star Route 1, Box 249, Woodville, TX 75979. Phone (409) 429–3491.

Village Creek State Park. The newest recreational park in the Big Thicket region is Village Creek State Park, located on a pretty stretch of the namesake stream in Hardin County. Facilities and services include campsites with electrical hookups and water, primitive camp sites, canoeing, fishing, fish-cleaning stations, swimming, picnicking areas, a group shelter for family reunions and conferences, trailer dump station, and ten miles of scenic hiking trails.

Village Creek swimming can be a world-beater. Wildlife observed in the 943-acre park includes red foxes, bobcats, beavers, minks, armadillos, raccoons, a variety of turtles, and abundant birdlife. Signs of alligators have been noted.

To reach the park, go to Lumberton, which is ten miles north of Interstate 10 on U.S. 96, and watch for directional signs.

For information and reservations: Village Creek State Park, P.O. Box 8575, Lumberton, TX 77711. Phone (409) 755–7322.

Lake Livingston State Recreation Area. A large and lovely complex on a major Texas lake located six miles southwest of Livingston on FM 3128. Varying fees for campsites with water and electricity, sites with just water, and shelters. Showers available; boat ramps, hiking trails, store. Open all year. Information: (409) 365–2201.

National Forests. All of the four national forests that touch the Big Thicket region contain numerous camping facilities. For the latest information on them, call (409) 639- 8501, or write to National Forests, Homer Garrison Federal Building, 701 North First Street, Lufkin, TX 75901.

Sea Rim State Park. Texas 87 between Sabine Pass and High Island; Twelve miles from Sabine Pass. Near, but not in, the Big Thicket region. Varying fees for beach camping, sites with electricity and water hookups. Annual state park pass or entrance fee required. Reservations available. Open all year. Information: (409) 971–2559.

Fishing

Anglers go after catfish, bass, crappie, drum, sunfish, mullet, and buffalo in the nine waterways of the Big Thicket. To bait their hooks, they seine for gizzard shad, threadfin shad, carp, and blackspot shiners. All told, ninety-eight known species of fish swim in Big Thicket waters. Most of them ain't worth batterin' and fryin' but some are wonderfully toothsome and tasty. For the seven most popular fishes, named above, here are the likely fishing spots, according to official records.

Pine Island Bayou—yellow bullhead catfish, channel

catfish, flathead catfish, freshwater drum, smallmouth buffalo, warmouth, bluegill, redear sunfish, largemouth bass, white crappie, black crappie, white bass. Baitfish: gizzard shad, threadfin shad, carp. Pine Island Bayou has a total of fifty-six species of fish on record.

Neches Drain (sloughs and swamps that drain the Neches River channel)—blue catfish, yellow bullhead, channel catfish, flathead catfish, freshwater drum, striped mullet, smallmouth buffalo, bigmouth buffalo, black buffalo, warmouth, bluegill, redear sunfish, largemouth bass, white crappie, black crappie, white bass. Baitfish: gizzard shad, threadfin shad, carp, blackspot shiner. The Neches Drains have a total of eighty-eight species of fish on record, the largest number of species in Big Thicket waterways.

Neches River—channel catfish, freshwater drum, striped mullet, warmouth, bluegill, redear sunfish, largemouth bass, white crappie, black crappie. Baitfish: Gizzard shad, threadfin shad, blackspot shiner. The Neches River has a total of sixty-nine species of fish on record.

Beech Creek—yellow bullhead catfish, largemouth bass, warmouth, bluegill. Baitfish: Blackspot shiner. Beech Creek has a total of thirty-eight species of fish on record.

Turkey Creek—largemouth bass, white crappie, black crappie, warmouth, bluegill, redear sunfish. Baitfish: none of the most popular kinds, but numerous species of minnows, perches, and sunfish. Turkey Creek has a total of thirty-three species of fish on record.

Hickory Creek—warmouth, bluegill. Baitfish: blackspot shiner. Hickory Creek has a total of thirty-five species of fish on record.

Big Sandy Creek—largemouth bass, yellow bullhead catfish, channel catfish, warmouth, bluegill. Baitfish: blackspot shiner. Big Sandy Creek has a total of thirty-nine species of fish on record.

Menard Creek—largemouth bass, white crappie, warmouth, bluegill. Baitfish: none of the most popular kinds, but several species of minnows, perches, and sunfish. Menard Creek has a total of twenty-eight species of fish on record.

Village Creek—largemouth bass, black crappie, yellow

bullhead catfish, channel catfish, striped mullet, warmouth, bluegill, redear sunfish. Baitfish: none of the most popular kinds, but numerous species of minnows, perches, and sunfishes. Village Creek has a total of forty-seven species of fish on record.

And a roundup of Big Thicket species of fish: one paddlefish, one bowfin, seven catfish, one drum, one eel, three gars, two herrings, five killifishes, two lampreys, one live bearer, twenty-three minnows, three mullets, thirteen perches, one pike, one pirate perch, four silversides, one sole, one snake eel, nine suckers, sixteen sunfish and two temperate bass.

Licenses, laws and regulations of the State of Texas apply to fishing in Big Thicket waters.

Canoeing

Rapidly growing in popularity, canoeing in the Big Thicket offers a recreational experience different from any other.

Three waterways—the Neches River, Village Creek, and Pine Island Bayou—provide canoeists several choices of environment and activity. The Neches River flows fifty-four miles through the National Preserve, and its side trips are so appealing that a float can easily add on miles and time. For convenience, planners often split the Neches River run into four sections. For Village Creek, one float covers thirty-seven miles, a shorter one twists for only about seven miles. To paddle and portage Pine Island Bayou, you can plan on a forty-nine-mile outing.

Neches River

This historic and often scenic river flows south about 420 miles from two farmland seeps near Chandler, Texas, to the Gulf of Mexico near Port Arthur. After passing a northern reservoir, Lake Palestine, south of Chandler, it winds through piney woods until reaching the Big Thicket region. Farther along, Dam B impounds the flow at Steinhagen Lake. At the dam, the river becomes part of the Big Thicket National Preserve until it reaches Beaumont.

Sandbars along the fifty-four-mile stretch make interesting primitive campgrounds and day-use stops. For camping, you'll need a free permit from a ranger station or headquarters of the National Park Service.

The Neches River can be a deep and tricky waterway, and it's important that canoeists take safety precautions.

Section One of a split river run covers fourteen miles, from Dam B down to FM 1013. Put in at a boat ramp on the west side of the river at Town Bluff community—there's a small fee—or a ramp on the east side at East End Park managed by the U.S. Corps of Engineers.

Allow five to six hours for canoeing this section, which displays scenic high sandstone and iron ore bluffs during the last several miles. Sandbars often grace the shoreline. Wildlife: moderate. Channel: wide, open, no hazards, but a small gravel bar extends across the channel at River Mile 96. Watch for the River Mile 95 sign so you'll know the gravel bar is just ahead.

A private ramp will be found on the east side of the river after passing southward under FM 1013. The owner charges a fee for use.

Section Two of the Neches River run goes for forty miles from FM 1013 to U.S. 96. Plan for twenty hours in your canoe.

This section is a fairly wild stretch of the Neches, with large sandbars in the first twenty-five miles offering good campsites. The last half of this float borders the Jack Gore Baygall and Neches Bottom Units of the Big Thicket National Preserve, and is considered the most remote segment of the river. It offers excellent side trips to serene oxbow lakes and backwater cypress sloughs.

Don't fail to slip east into Deep Slough, about a mile-and-a-half past the Hardin County Park. Primeval-type bottomland forest, a great haven for wildlife, lines Deep Slough.

The Hardin County Park offers primitive camping. Channel conditions: wide, open, no known hazards at this writing. At times an upstream wind can make canoeing more strenuous than usual.

At U.S. 96, a public boat ramp provides year-round access.

Section Three covers sixteen miles, from U.S. 96 to Lakeview. The land here is often swampy, but you should find a few sandbars for camping if you need to set up along the way.

Again, the best sights unfold in the adjoining sloughs and oxbows. This section shows civilization creeping up the river from its southern segment. Look out for jet boats and water skiers.

At River Mile 38, a private improved boat ramp on a bayou near the Lakeview community provides access. It's on the east bank.

Section Four covers ten miles, from Lakeview to Beaumont. It's about a five-hour float. The National Park Service says, "No camping along the Neches River past Lakeview. Day use only."

The upper two-thirds of this section wind and curl down to Scatterman Lake, about a mile-and-a-half past River Mile 33. For wildlife habitat, exploring, and fishing, Scatterman is worth a turnoff westward. Back on the river, another mile-plus southward, the Neches intersects with Pine Island Bayou. Take the bayou for a mile or so to Cook's Lake, a prime spot to experience a sense of remoteness.

A boat ramp awaits your usage across the river from Pine Island Bayou. Look out for them jet boats and water skiers again.

Village Creek

Flowing through the heart of the Big Thicket, Village Creek angles past dense forests and cypress swamps, at times requiring canoeists to duck overhanging branches and to portage around log jams. The bordering plant life is remarkable for its diversity, just the kind of cover preferred by myriad forms of wildlife. Little wonder that Village Creek has become a favorite of area canoeists.

Averaging twenty to thirty feet wide, Village Creek usually has water levels sufficient for canoeing, but dry summer months make some portaging likely. To add to the appeal of spring, fall, and mild winter canoeing, the sum-

Canoeists love Village Creek's wide places and white sandbars amidst dense woods.

mer months lay a blanket of heat over the creek's way, creating a paradise for insects.

North of the community of Village Mills on U.S. 69/287, the same waters take the name Big Sandy Creek, flowing down from the vicinity of the Alabama-Coushatta Indian Reservation.

The National Park Service suggests a thirty-seven-mile float from U.S. 69/287, through the southern "boot" of the Turkey Creek Unit, past a meeting with Beech Creek, on to the Larsen Sandyland Sanctuary, and a final run to the Neches River. All along the way, white sandbars tempt the lazy canoeist to pause and ponder.

Spots for takeouts include the crossing at FM 418 between Kountze and Silsbee, the crossing of Texas 327 at the Larsen Sandyland Sanctuary, and a Texas Parks and Wildlife boat ramp at the U.S. 96 crossing.

"Because of its remoteness, outstanding scenic qualities, and lack of impoundments," says a National Park Service leaflet, "Village Creek retains wild and pristine characteristics."

A shorter float about seven miles in length, from FM 418 to Larsen Sandyland Sanctuary, wiggles through a segment of dense forest typical of the Big Thicket.

Pine Island Bayou

Laziest creek in the Big Thicket—that's Pine Island Bayou. Or so some canoeists say, especially those who like a slow flow. Here's what a National Park Service canoeist had to report:

"Scenic and popular . . . the almost impenetrable thicket holds a remarkably wide variety of plant life . . . Much of the plant and animal life is rare or endangered, thus nature is in delicate balance throughout this area . . . periodic sand and gravel bars (for camping day use) . . . "

Problems here? Probably. This bayou narrows down quite a bit at spots. Overhanging brush and limbs can be bothersome. During dry weather spells, the upper reaches of the creek don't hold much water. During rainy periods, the main channel can be difficult to define. And during the summer, heat and insects deserve the general cussing they get. However, good canoeists say the rewards of this creek far outstrip the potential aggravations.

Pine Island Bayou shuffles along forty-nine miles from the crossing of FM 770, two miles southwest of Saratoga, to its merger with the Neches River above Beaumont.

Sloping roads for takeouts are usually found at the crossings of County Road, three miles southeast of Sour Lake; and Texas 105, six miles east of Sour Lake. You'll find a boat ramp at the crossing of U.S. 96/69/287 at the northwest city limits of Beaumont.

Important! Because of the considerable distance from FM 770 to the takeout points—by the time you're reading this, the Texas 326 crossing, twenty-one miles downstream, may be another one—plan your float carefully. Don't get caught at sundown at a place where you don't want to spend the night.

All canoeists! Use all safety precautions wherever you canoe in the Big Thicket. Take no undue risks. Know what you're doing.

Local Canoe Rentals

The information presented in this list represents conditions at press-time for this *Guide*. Rates and arrangements—and even companies in existence—may change.

Eastex Canoe Rentals
5865 Cole Road
Beaumont, TX 77706
(409) 892–3600
$15 per day rental
Will arrange shuttles

Canoe Rentals-Silsbee
Old Beaumont
Highway
(409) 385–6241
$15 per day rental
Will arrange shuttles

Craig Davis
Rt. 2, Box 445
Kountze, TX 77625
(409) 246-4817
$15 per day rental
Will arrange shuttles

H&H Boat Dock and Marina
U.S. 190 near FM 92 junction
Steinhagen Reservoir
(409) 283–3257
$10 per day rental
No shuttle service available

The Piney Woods Canoe
Company
P.O. Box 1994
Kountze, TX 77625
(409) 274–5892
$17 per day rental
$14 per day with four
or more boats
Will arrange shuttles

Village Creek Canoe Rental
FM 418
P.O. Box 281
Kountze, TS 77625
(409) 246-4481
$15 per day rental
$12 per day with four
or more boats
Limited shuttle service

Hunting

Hunting here requires a valid State of Texas hunting license and, if done in specified units of the Big Thicket National Preserve, a hunting permit issued by the National

Park Service Headquarters of the National Preserve for a particular season.

Private hunting clubs lease or own tracts where members only hunt. For information on these and other hunting possibilities outside the National Preserve, contact the State Parks and Wildlife Service in Beaumont, or a Chamber of Commerce in the area of your interest.

In the Big Thicket National Preserve, hunting permits are issued for specific areas in the following units: Beaumont Unit, Big Sandy Creek Unit, Beech Creek Unit, and Jack Gore Baygall Unit. Permits allow the following animals to be taken: white-tailed deer, squirrel, rabbit, feral hog, migratory game birds, and game birds.

Legal weapons include the following: bow and arrow, shotgun, .22 rimfire cartridge rifle, muzzle-loaded rifle, and smooth-bore muzzle-loaded weapons.

For each hunting season, the National Park Service issues a limited number of permits for each of the six units. Any person who wants a permit must be present to register for the permit. Children aged twelve and under don't need a permit.

Interested persons should contact NPS Headquarters, (409) 839–2689, for all current data and a list of about twenty regulations.

NOTE: Some of the listings in this chapter may have changed since being compiled.

9 Nearby Natural Spots

The Roy E. Larsen Sandyland Sanctuary

This is the prime example of the peculiarity known as arid sandylands in the Big Thicket. Peculiar? Well, it has many of the qualities of the American southwestern desert, yet it receives rain galore and typical Big Thicket humidity throughout the year.

Prickly pear cactus and yucca thrive among scrubby oaks and scattered longleaf pines. Orchids, carnivorous plants, and more than three hundred kinds of wildflowers soften the look of the sandy floor. The sandy ridges grade into three very different ecosystems within a few steps of each other. And to complete the puzzle, an arctic lichen pops out of the sand hither and yon. Strange!

The three ecosystems interspersed with the arid sandylands here include Baygall, Oak-gum Floodplain, and Beech-Magnolia-Loblolly settings. See Chapter 2 for more information on the Arid Sandylands ecosystem.

Village Creek curls along the western boundary of the sanctuary, which covers 2,178 acres and offers about six miles of trails for hiking and nature study. It's owned and managed by the Texas Nature Conservancy, a private, non-profit conservation organization.

Enter the sanctuary on Texas 327 about two-and-a-half miles west of Silsbee. Or, if you're traveling west to east, take Texas 327 south of Kountze and head eastward for a couple miles. Just as you cross the bridge over Village Creek, look to your left— the north side of the highway— and you'll see the sanctuary sign.

The original land for the sanctuary was given by Temple-Inland and Time, Inc., to honor Roy E. Larsen, an executive of Time, Inc. Additional acres were later contributed by Gulf States Utilities Company.

Open to the public during daylight hours, the sanctuary has a No Camping rule. Other prohibitions in this delicate environment: no fires, hunting, wheeled vehicles, pets, or horses; no collecting plants or animals or disturbing the natural features. Visitors are asked to please stay on the trails.

For more information on this remarkable area, contact the manager at P.O. Box 909, Silsbee, TX 77656; or phone (409) 385-4135 or (409) 385-0445.

Sea Rim State Park

Fairly far—say, sixty miles or so—from the Big Thicket's southern border of Pine Island Bayou, Sea Rim State Park provides interesting insights into the relationships between forest, prairie, and coast.

At Sea Rim, you can see the meeting point of tidal marshlands and the open Gulf. Wildlife familiar to both disparate ecosystems of the Big Thicket and the saltwater coast overlap here: raccoon, rabbit, mink, skunk, opossum, nutria, river otter, and alligator. Plus, there's a fabulous array of bird life.

Bones of prehistoric animals—mastodon and mammoth, to name just two—that inhabited the Big Thicket tens of thousands of years ago are collected by scientists on the beach around Sea Rim. After all, the waters now known as the Gulf of Mexico once covered the Big Thicket, not only once but four times.

Sea Rim State Park is located ten miles west of Sabine Pass, which is about twenty-two miles south of Port Arthur. Its 15,109 acres include more than five miles of coastline, plus boat trails into the marsh, observation platforms, and a boardwalk 3,640 feet in length—the Gambusia Trail—where visitors get a close-up acquaintance with marshland ecology.

No telling how many thousands of ducks, geese, and other waterfowl concentrate in the area during the fall and winter months. You can fish, camp, paddle your pirogue or canoe in the park, and photograph wildlife from the various platforms and blinds.

For more information: Park Superintendent, Sea Rim State Park, P.O. Box 1066, Sabine Pass, TX 77655. Phone: (409) 971-2559.

The National Forests

Four huge national forests touch upon the Big Thicket region and offer a tremendous range of recreational facilities and nature-appreciation possibilities.

Angelina National Forest sits atop the Neches River and the Angelina River on the northern rim of the Big Thicket. Its 153,175 acres contain seven camping and recreational areas, including Bouton Lake, Boykin Springs, and various locations on Sam Rayburn Reservoir.

Sabine National Forest, which borders Toledo Bend Reservoir where upper East Texas meets Louisiana, contains superb mixed hardwood-evergreen woodlands. Six camping and recreational sites dot its 160,609 acres. The Indian Mounds hiking trail ranks with the best in East Texas.

Sam Houston National Forest tips the western limits of the Big Thicket region around Cleveland, Coldspring, and Livingston. The Lone Star hiking trail traverses the national forest for 140 miles, and part of it—27 miles on the southeastern leg—qualifies for National Recreation Trail status. This national forest contains 161,508 acres.

A fourth national forest in East Texas, **Davy Crockett,** lies between Lufkin and Crockett. It encompasses extensive recreational facilities around Ratcliff Lake, in the central portion, and a large game management area.

Among the facilities found in the national forests, depending on the various recreational areas, are picnicking, camping, sanitary facilities, drinking water, swimming, boating, boat launching ramps, fishing, and hiking trails. Not all recreational areas have all facilities. Fees are charged for the use of some facilities.

National Forest Service policies allow hunting and fishing in accordance with Texas state law.

"Dead out"—that's the way to leave any campfires. For additional information, write or phone: National Forests, Homer Garrison Federal Building, 701 N. First St., Lufkin, TX 75901. (409) 639–8501.

Woodland Trails

One of the spectacular sights—and smells—of the Big Thicket region, maybe of the entire southeastern United States, unfolds at Wild Azalea Canyons at the peak of the bloom.

Nearby Natural Spots

That short period usually comes around April 1, give or take a few days depending on the preceding winter and spring. If conditions reach a peak, deep ravines here glow and quiver with thousands of wild azaleas flowering and perfuming the surrounding longleaf pine woods. Some years, nature provides more and better blooms than in other years.

Wild Azalea Canyons is one of fifteen pockets of East Texas natural beauty set aside by large timber companies for public enjoyment. Their industry association, the Texas Forestry Association, coordinates the Woodland Trails program and provides maps on request. Nine of the trails are found in the Big Thicket region.

The **Wild Azalea Canyons Trail** is located in Newton County, about twelve miles from Newton. Go 4.4 miles on Texas 87 north of Newton, turn east on FM 1414, then drive 6.7 miles to an unpaved road with a large sign. Turn as the arrow points and go 1.8 miles to the trail's parking area. Note: the ravines get steep and the footing gets gravelly and uncertain. But if you catch the azaleas at the right time in a good year, the place sticks in your memory forever.

Newton County also contains the **Sylvan Trail**. The half-mile walk wanders through a picturesque growth of loblolly pines. Two old logging roads add interest. Located four miles southeast of Newton, the Sylvan Trail begins opposite a roadside park on U.S. 190.

If you find yourself in Jasper County with a hunch to hike, try the Sawmill Trail or the Old River Trail.

The **Sawmill Trail**, south of Zavalla off Texas 63, takes off from three trailheads and makes a fancy Y for about five-and-a-half miles. One trailhead begins at the town of Aldridge, one at Boykin Springs, another at Bouton Lake Campground.

Old River Trail follows an abandoned railroad into a hardwood bottomland of the Angelina River. The trailhead appears after you drive on an unpaved road that intersects FM 1747, which intersects U.S. 190. Follow the signs. The trail is an interesting walk of one-and-a-half miles.

Polk County contains three Woodland Trails.

The endangered red-cockaded woodpecker made nesting holes amidst one hundred-year-old pines on the **Longleaf Pine Trail,** located three miles east of Camden on FM 62. The trail can also be reached by driving east from Corrigan on U.S. 287 and watching for the turnoff on FM 62. The trail angles through woods for about two miles.

Bull Creek Trail, located eight-and-a-half miles west of Corrigan on U.S. 287, features large oaks, gums, and magnolias on a path that follows Bull Creek, a spring-fed stream. Trail length is one-and-a-half miles.

Moscow Trail, a short distance south of the town of Moscow on U.S. 59, combines a short walk of one-half mile with a longer walk, a mile-and-a-half, along Long King Creek, a stream named for a famous Indian chief. Tall pines spike the mixed hardwood-evergreen forest.

In Tyler County, three miles east of Woodville off U.S. 190, the **Dogwood Trail** doesn't have many showy dogwoods, but it does have splendid beech trees, rare flowers like the yellow dog's-tooth violet, which is not a violet at all, and uncommon surprises like May-apple colonies. "Tootl'em Creek" and several sandy-bed feeders give the trail a postcard aspect. Tootl'em is actually Theuvenin Creek, but a lot of old-timers slurred their words. The length of the trail is one-and-a-half miles.

Another clear-running stream borders part of the **Big Creek Trail** in San Jacinto County, west of Shepherd on Forest Service Road 217, which intersects Texas 150, which intersects U.S. 59. Just turn west at Shepherd and you'll find it. Big Creek Trail boasts a loop four-and-a-half miles long.

Six additional East Texas Trails, outside the Big Thicket region, complete the Woodland Trails program of the Texas Forestry Association. For additional information and de-

A pausing spot on the trail beside Tootl'em Creek.

tailed directions, write or phone the association at Box 1488, Lufkin, TX 75901. Phone: (409) 632–8733.

Special Places in the Forest

Special Places in the Forest is the title of an environmental program of Champion International, a corporation with vast timber holdings in the region of the Big Thicket and elsewhere. The program sets aside ten areas of varying sizes and environmental features for tours usually restricted to nature groups, student classes, and scientific teams. Six of the ten areas lie within the Big Thicket region.

The **Kickapoo Creek** preserve contains 320 acres in Polk and Trinity counties. It's noted for rock outcroppings that might have resulted from a long-ago earthquake.

Another Polk County preserve, the fourteen-acre **Carter Sand and Water Stop,** features a spring-fed bog and an impressive example of Longleaf Sandylands.

A third special place in Polk County, the **Beaver Pond** offers trails to several ponds built by beavers since about 1970. This preserve covers forty acres.

Westward in Walker County, **Dillard Creek** preserve displays a geological fault that pushed huge boulders, petrified wood, fossils, and lignite outcroppings to the surface along a stream corridor. A pioneer crossing of the stream dates back nearly one hundred years. The preserve follows the stream for some 270 acres.

Down in Liberty County, **Batiste Creek** creases a three hundred–acre area of hardwood-canopied swamps. Champion says the area has lain "undisturbed by man for decades."

Up in Tyler County, the special place is a seventy-nine–acre site called the **Beech Magnolia Canyons.**

In addition to those preserves in the immediate Big Thicket region, Champion has set aside the **Oyster Reefs and the Blue Heron Rookery** in Trinity County; the **Apolonia Trail** in Grimes County; and the mission of **Nuestra Señora de la Purísima Concepción de los Hainai,** a historical mission site in Nacogdoches County.

To arrange for tours or visits, contact: Special Places Coordinator, Texas Timberlands Region, Champion International, Box 191, Huntsville, TX 77340. Phone: (409) 291–3381.

Trail Notes

• Two river otters swam under his canoe while he was exploring a slough off the Neches River, James Overstreet reports. They surfaced on the other side of the craft and swam on their backs, watching him, seeming to smile, until they disappeared around a nearby bend. This rare event happened last February, a month of the mating season for river otters. James is a Hardin County thicketeer who likes water-roving.

• Don't drive through a rain-filled mudhole on a backwoods road without testing it first. A lot of those mudholes will gulp a wheel up to the axle. And there you're stuck, nine miles from nowhere.

• A *Houston Post* columnist recently expressed disappointment in the fall colors of the Big Thicket. He came over from the big city and spent the afternoon on the highways around the Kountze and Saratoga area. That was an uninformed thing to do. Richer color can be found farther north, in Tyler, Jasper, Newton, and Polk counties, where more beeches and sugar maples live. He was right in one repect. Fall color in the Big Thicket doesn't smack you with a wide vista of brilliant reds and golds, as in New England. Some newcomers expect that. But the woods here crowd up with more kinds of competing trees and shrubs than in New England. Also, the bulldozer takes a heavy toll in the forests year after year, except for the woods protected by the Big Thicket National Preserve. And even those woods are just now recovering from generations of exploitation. Fall color in the Big Thicket can be expressed in a single splendid specimen here and there, or in patches of colorful trees, or along a shoreline where massed hues shimmer in reflection. The sight is no less beautiful than a long row of Vermont maples, just different—more like an impressionistic painting than a picture postcard.

The best places to find fall color in the Thicket are on

A fallen leaf, caught by pine needles and backlit by the sun, reveals dynamic patterns of venation.

borders of woods and ponds and backroads, usually about the third week of November. Much depends on the number of cold nights and warm days and whether the winds blow hard enough to strip leaves from limbs. The color in the leaves has been there all year, but greened over by the tree's production of chlorophyll. When fall arrives, the chemical factory in the tree shuts down and the green chlorophyll jacketing the leaves dissolves, exposing the various shades of reds and yellows that were there all along. Red leaves indicate the presence of a sugary material, saccarhum. Yellow leaves tell of carotene.

The trees and shrubs of color in the Thicket include sugar maple, swamp maple, box-elder (also a maple), red oak, white oak, sweetgum, most of the many hawthorns, the sumacs, black gum and tupelo, dogwood, American beech, the various hickories, various blueberry shrubs, cottonwood, black willow, hop-hornbeam, river birch, paw-paw, Ohio buckeye, the various ashes, grancy graybeard, and sassafras. And don't forget vines like poison-ivy and Virginia creeper, both real fall showoffs. The way to see fall color in the Thicket is first in early morning fog, with all the colors smeared and softened, then when the sun lifts the fog and sharpens the same colors and makes prisms of the dew on the leaves.

• Fall moves down from the north, spring comes up from the south, each at the rate of about 17.25 miles per day. A fellow named Hopkins figured that out; hence the scientific community named his calculations Hopkins's Bioclimatic Law. If he was right, it means that after spring arrives one day, say, at Pine Island Bayou where it crosses U.S. 69/287, the next day it moves to about Kountze, then the following day to about Hickory Creek, then up to Woodville, and on beyond the rim of the Big Thicket toward Zavalla. Just reverse the order for fall. The points are conjectural, of course. But we're talking principle here.

• With all eyes on fall color in the leaves each year, the spring color takes a hind seat. I doubt if any area in the United States or Canada can match the many shades of green that appear in the Thicket's new leaves. One April morning, on a drive along U.S. 190 from Woodville to Livingston, I pulled off the road and counted eighteen different shades of green in the treeline bordering the highway. Magnificent! The colors spanned the spectrum from dark, almost black, green through emerald and smoky green to the electric chartreuse of beech trees. The latter shade is the most striking green in all nature.

A hermit's hut in the remote woods? Nah, just the root maze of an old tree blown over.

• Always take a pocket magnifier on a walk in the Thicket. Much of the action and beauty of a field or woods occur on a small scale. The weed Ludwigia, for example—I know of no common name—makes a seedbox whose design and construction will astound and mesmerize any artisan, cabinetmaker, or connoisseur who views it through a magnifier.

• A smart woods-walker glances often at the path immediately ahead when leaf litter covers the ground. Roots jutting across the path, all but hidden under the litter, trip the unwary and can send the stroller sprawling.

• Visitors frequently call and ask me where to stay and eat in the Thicket communities. I stay at the Beaumont Hilton. The facilities and services there impress me as excellent, and it often offers some kind of special rate on weekends. As for eats, I believe it all depends on who's doing the cooking and who's cleaned up, no matter what the name of the restaurant. I like to eat at The Homestead in Hillister, which is open on Friday and Saturday nights and Sunday noons. The fried catfish there equals the best I've eaten anywhere. Other dishes are tasty, too. The owners, Otho and Emily Sumner, are great folks.

Don't hurry or scurry on a Thicket outing. This pond invites a contemplative moment.

Appendixes

Checklist, Birds by Habitat

Some Birds to Look for in Mixed Evergreen-Hardwood forests

( ) sharp-shinned hawk (spring, fall, winter)
( ) Cooper's hawk (all seasons)
( ) merlin (summer)
( ) American woodcock (winter)
( ) yellow-billed cuckoo (spring, summer, fall)
( ) eastern screech owl (all seasons)
( ) barred owl (all seasons)
( ) long-eared owl (spring)
( ) ruby-throated hummingbird (spring, summer)
( ) red-headed woodpecker (all seasons)
( ) red-bellied woodpecker (all seasons)
( ) yellow-bellied sapsucker (spring, fall, winter)
( ) downy woodpecker (all seasons)
( ) pileated woodpecker (all seasons)
( ) great crested flycatcher (spring, summer)
( ) yellow-bellied flycatcher (spring, fall)
( ) Acadian flycatcher (spring, summer, fall)
( ) eastern wood pewee (spring, summer, fall)
( ) blue jay (all seasons)
( ) Carolina chickadee (all seasons)
( ) tufted titmouse (all seasons)
( ) white-breasted nuthatch (all seasons)
( ) brown creeper (spring, winter)
( ) Carolina wren (all seasons)
( ) winter wren (spring, fall, winter)
( ) wood thrush (all seasons)
( ) hermit thrush (spring, winter)
( ) Swainson's thrush (spring, fall)
( ) gray-cheeked thrush (spring, winter)
( ) veery (spring)
( ) blue-gray gnatcatcher (all seasons)
( ) golden-crowned kinglet (spring, winter)

( ) northern ruby-crowned kinglet (spring, fall, winter)
( ) cedar waxwing (spring, winter)
( ) yellow-throated vireo (spring, summer, winter)
( ) solitary vireo (spring, fall, winter)
( ) warbling vireo (summer)
( ) red-eyed vireo (spring, summer, fall)
( ) black-and-white warbler (spring, summer, fall)
( ) prothonotary warbler (spring, summer, fall)
( ) Swainson's warbler (spring, summer, fall)
( ) worm-eating warbler (spring, summer, fall)
( ) orange-crowned warbler (spring, winter)
( ) northern parula warbler (spring, summer, fall)
( ) magnolia warbler (spring)
( ) Blackburnian warbler (spring)
( ) yellow-throated warbler (spring, summer, fall)
( ) blackpoll warbler (spring)
( ) ovenbird (spring, fall)
( ) Louisiana waterthrush (all seasons)
( ) Kentucky warbler (spring, summer, fall)
( ) hooded warbler (spring, summer, fall)
( ) American redstart (all seasons)
( ) scarlet tanager (spring)
( ) summer tanager (spring, summer, fall)
( ) evening grosbeak (spring)
( ) purple finch (winter)
( ) American goldfinch (spring, fall, winter)
( ) white-crowned sparrow (spring, winter)
( ) fox sparrow (winter)

Some Birds to Look for in Open Fields with Scattered Trees

( ) cattle egret (all seasons)
( ) Canada goose (winter)
( ) snow goose (winter)
( ) turkey vulture (all seasons)
( ) black vulture (all seasons)
( ) red-tailed hawk (all seasons)
( ) American kestrel (spring, fall, winter)
( ) killdeer (all seasons)
( ) Inca dove (all seasons)

( ) mourning dove (all seasons)
( ) great horned owl (all seasons)
( ) chuck-will's-widow (spring, summer)
( ) common nighthawk (summer, fall)
( ) northern flicker (all seasons)
( ) red-headed woodpecker (all seasons)
( ) eastern kingbird (spring, summer)
( ) scissor-tailed flycatcher (spring, summer, fall)
( ) purple martin (spring, summer, fall)
( ) American crow (all seasons)
( ) fish crow (all seasons)
( ) northern mockingbird (all seasons)
( ) American robin (spring, summer, winter)
( ) eastern bluebird (all seasons)
( ) loggerhead shrike (all seasons)
( ) European starling (all seasons)
( ) house sparrow (all seasons)
( ) red-winged blackbird (all seasons)
( ) orchard oriole (spring, summer, fall)
( ) northern oriole (spring, fall)
( ) Brewer's blackbird (winter)
( ) common grackle (all seasons)
( ) brown-headed cowbird (all seasons)

Some Birds to Look for in Open Skies

( ) Canada goose (winter)
( ) snow goose (winter)
( ) turkey vulture (all seasons)
( ) black vulture (all seasons)
( ) American swallow-tailed kite (spring, summer)
( ) Mississippi kite (spring, winter)
( ) red-tailed hawk (all seasons)
( ) red-shouldered hawk (all seasons)
( ) broad-winged hawk (spring, summer, fall)
( ) bald eagle (winter)
( ) chuck-will's-widow (spring, summer)
( ) common nighthawk (summer, fall)
( ) chimney swift (spring, summer, fall)
( ) purple martin (spring, summer, fall)
( ) tree swallow (spring, fall)

( ) bank swallow (spring, summer, fall)
( ) northern rough-winged swallow (spring, summer, fall)
( ) barn swallow (spring, summer)
( ) cliff swallow (spring, fall)

Some Birds to Look for around Open Water

( ) horned grebe (winter)
( ) western grebe (winter)
( ) pied-billed grebe (all seasons)
( ) American white pelican (summer, fall)
( ) double-crested cormorant (spring, fall)
( ) anhinga (all seasons)
( ) ringed-billed gull (winter)
( ) Franklin's gull (winter)
( ) Caspian tern (winter)
( ) Forster's tern (winter)
( ) black tern (spring)
( ) black-bellied whistling duck (summer)
( ) mallard (spring, winter)
( ) mottled duck (summer)
( ) blue-winged teal (spring)
( ) wood duck (all seasons)
( ) American swallow-tailed kite (spring, summer)
( ) northern harrier (winter)
( ) belted kingfish (all seasons)
( ) eastern phoebe (spring, fall, winter)
( ) tree swallow (spring, fall)
( ) bank swallow (spring, summer, fall)
( ) northern rough-winged swallow (spring, summer, fall)
( ) cliff swallow (spring, fall)
( ) fish crow (all seasons)
( ) northern oriole (spring, fall)

Some Birds to Look for in Upland Pine Forests

( ) sharp-shinned hawk (spring, fall, winter)
( ) Cooper's hawk (all seasons)
( ) broad-winged hawk (spring, summer, fall)
( ) merlin falcon (summer)

( ) American woodcock (winter)
( ) yellow-billed cuckoo (spring, summer, fall)
( ) eastern screech owl (all seasons)
( ) great horned owl (all seasons)
( ) northern flicker (all seasons)
( ) red-bellied woodpecker (all seasons)
( ) yellow-bellied sapsucker (spring, fall, winter)
( ) downy woodpecker (all seasons)
( ) pileated woodpecker (all seasons)
( ) great crested flycatcher (spring, summer)
( ) eastern wood pewee (spring, summer, fall)
( ) blue jay (all seasons)
( ) American crow (all seasons)
( ) Carolina chickadee (all seasons)
( ) tufted titmouse (all seasons)
( ) red-breasted nuthatch (spring, summer, winter)
( ) brown-headed nuthatch (all seasons)
( ) brown creeper (winter, spring)

Some Birds to Look for in Marshes
( ) green-backed heron (spring, summer)
( ) least bittern (summer)
( ) common snipe (winter)
( ) yellow warbler (spring)

Some Birds to Look for in Grasslands
( ) northern harrier (winter)
( ) eastern meadowlark (all seasons)
( ) savannah sparrow (fall, winter)
( ) grasshopper sparrow (winter)
( ) Henslow's sparrow (winter)
( ) LeConte's sparrow (winter)
( ) vesper sparrow (winter)
( ) lark sparrow (winter)

Some Birds to Look for along the Shorelines
( ) great blue heron (all seasons)
( ) little blue heron (spring, summer)
( ) cattle egret (all seasons)
( ) great egret (all seasons)

Birds

( ) snowy egret (spring, summer, winter)
( ) tricolored heron (summer)
( ) green-backed heron (spring, summer)
( ) yellow-crowned night heron (spring, summer)
( ) American bittern (spring, fall, winter)
( ) wood stork (summer)
( ) white ibis (summer, fall)
( ) mottled duck (summer)
( ) blue-winged teal (spring)
( ) killdeer (all seasons)
( ) spotted sandpiper (all seasons)
( ) ruddy turnstone (winter)
( ) northern waterthrush (spring)
( ) Louisiana waterthrush (all seasons)
( ) common yellowthroat (all seasons)
( ) red-winged blackbird (all seasons)
( ) song sparrow (winter)

Some Birds to Look for in the Thickets

( ) northern bobwhite (all seasons)
( ) common snipe (winter)
( ) mourning dove (all seasons)
( ) greater roadrunner (all seasons)
( ) ruby-throated hummingbird (spring, summer)
( ) rufous hummingbird (spring, winter)
( ) eastern phoebe (spring, fall, winter)
( ) house wren (spring, fall, winter)
( ) winter wren (spring, fall, winter)
( ) Bewick's wren (winter)
( ) northern mockingbird (all seasons)
( ) gray catbird (spring, fall, winter)
( ) brown thrasher (all seasons)
( ) veery (all seasons)
( ) white-eyed vireo (all seasons)
( ) blue-winger warbler (spring)
( ) orange-crowned warbler (spring, winter)
( ) yellow warbler (spring)
( ) yellow-rumped warbler (spring, fall, winter)
( ) Blackburnian warbler (spring)
( ) prairie warbler (spring, summer)

( ) northern waterthrush (spring)
( ) common yellowthroat (all seasons)
( ) yellow-breasted chat (spring, summer, fall)
( ) Wilson's warbler (spring)
( ) orchard oriole (spring, summer, fall)
( ) northern cardinal (all seasons)
( ) rose-breasted grosbeak (spring)
( ) blue grosbeak (spring, summer, fall)
( ) indigo bunting (spring, summer, fall)
( ) painted bunting (spring, summer, fall)
( ) rufous-sided towhee (spring, fall, winter)
( ) northern junco (winter)
( ) field sparrow (winter)
( ) white-crowned sparrow (spring, winter)
( ) white-throated sparrow (spring, winter)
( ) fox sparrow (winter)
( ) Lincoln's sparrow (winter)
( ) swamp sparrow (winter)
( ) song sparrow (winter)

Appendix A

Checklist, Trees, Shrubs, and Vines

The plants listed below are mentioned in the text by their common names. This list serves as an introductory checklist for your field tally and also provides the scientific name of the species or genera for your reference and accuracy. Scientific names appear in italics. Bear in mind that common names vary from one locality to another, sometimes from one cousin to another, but the scientific name is the same the world over.

Also, remember that all checklists in this section reflect surveys by National Park Service scientists in only five of the fifteen units of the Big Thicket National Preserve— Beech Creek Unit, Loblolly Unit, Hickory Creek Savannah Unit, Big Sandy Creek Unit, and Turkey Creek Unit. No other units or natural areas in the Big Thicket region have been so surveyed for plants and wildlife and catalogued by the National Park Service at the time of this writing.

The lists of the five surveyed units can't be considered final and will change in the future as species relocate or disappear.

Trees

( ) southern sugar maple, *Acer barbatum*
( ) red maple, *A. rubrum*
( ) box-elder, *A. negundo*
( ) sugar maple, *A. saccharum*
( ) mimosa, *Albizia julibrissin*
( ) devil's walkingstick, *Aralia spinosa*
( ) river birch, *Betula nigra*
( ) muscle-tree or American hornbeam, *Carpinus caroliniana*
( ) water hickory, *Carya aquatica*
( ) bitternut hickory, *C. cordifurmis*
( ) pignut hickory, *C. glabra*

( ) swamp hickory, *C. leiodermis*
( ) shagbark hickory, *C. ovata*
( ) black hickory, *C. texana*
( ) mockernut hickory, *C. tomentosa*
( ) chinquapin, *Castanea pumila*
( ) cigar-tree, *Catalpa speciosa*
( ) Texas sugarberry, *Celtis laevigata*
( ) redbud, *Cercis canadensis*
( ) fringe tree, *Chionanthus virginica*
( ) trifoliate orange, *Citrus trifoliata*
( ) alternate-leaf dogwood, *Cornus alternifolia*
( ) flowering dogwood, *C. florida*
( ) English dogwood, *C. foemina*
( ) blueberry hawthorn, *Crataegus brachyacantha*
( ) cockspur, *C. crus-galli*
( ) parsley hawthorn, *C. marshallii*
( ) mayhaw, *C. opaca*
( ) pasture haw, *C. spathulata*
( ) green hawthorn, *C. viridus*
( ) titi, *Cyrilla racemiflora*
( ) common persimmon, *Diospyros virginiana*
( ) American beech, *Fagus grandifolia*
( ) white ash, *Fraxinus americana*
( ) water ash, *F. caroliniana*
( ) water locust, *Gleditsia aquatica*
( ) common honey locust, *G. tricanthos*
( ) two-winged silverbells, *Halesia diptera*
( ) American holly, *Ilex opaca*
( ) black walnut, *Juglans nigra*
( ) eastern red cedar, *Juniperus virginiana*
( ) crape-myrtle, *Lagerstroemia indica*
( ) sweetgum, *Liquidamber styraciflua*
( ) southern magnolia, *Magnolia grandiflora*
( ) sweet bay, *M. virginiana*
( ) chinaberry tree, *Melia azedarch*
( ) white mulberry, *Morus alba*
( ) red mulberry, *M. rubra*
( ) water tupelo, *Nyssa aquatica*
( ) black gum, *N. sylvatica*
( ) eastern hop-hornbeam, *Ostrya virginiana*

Appendix B

( ) red bay, *Persea borbonia*
( ) shortleaf pine, *Pinus echinata*
( ) slash pine, *P. elliottii*
( ) longleaf pine, *P. palustris*
( ) loblolly pine, *P. taeda*
Trees,   ( ) water elm, *Planera aquatica*
Shrubs, ( ) sycamore, *Platanus occidentalis*
Vines   ( ) eastern cottonwood, *Populus deltoides*
( ) Carolina cherry-laurel, *Prunus caroliniana*
( ) Mexican plum, *P. mexicana*
( ) black cherry, *P. serotina*
( ) flatwood plum, *P. umbellata*
( ) white oak, *Quercus alba*
( ) southern red oak, *Q. falcata*
( ) sandjack oak, *Q. incana*
( ) laurel-leaf oak, *Q. laurifolia*
( ) overcup oak, *Q. lyrata*
( ) blackjack oak, *Q. marilandica*
( ) water oak, *Q. nigra*
( ) willow oak, *Q. phellos*
( ) chestnut oak, *Q. prinus*
( ) Shumard oak, *Q. shumardii*
( ) post oak, *Q. stellata*
( ) black willow, *Salix nigra*
( ) Chinese tallow, *Sapium sebiferum*
( ) common sassafras, *Sassafras albidum*
( ) snow-bells, *Styrax americana*
( ) horse-sugar or sweet leaf, *Symplocus tinctoria*
( ) bald cypress, *Taxodium distichum*
( ) Florida basswood, *Tilia floridana*
( ) winged elm, *Ulmus alata*
( ) American elm, *U. Americana*
( ) slippery elm, *U. rubra*
( ) toothache-tree or Hercules-club, *Zanthoxylum clava-hercules*

Shrubs

( ) red buckeye, *Aesculus pavia*
( ) smooth alder, *Alnus serrulata*
( ) bastard indigo, *Amorpha fruticosa*

( ) panicled leadplant, *A. paniculata*
( ) common pawpaw, *Asimina parviflora*
( ) consumption-weed, *Baccharis halimifolia*
( ) sea myrtle, *B. salicina*
( ) ironweed, *Bumelia langinosa*
( ) American beauty-berry, *Callicarpa americana*
( ) downy chinquapin, *Castanea alnifolia*
( ) New Jersey tea, *Ceanothus americanus*
( ) button-bush, *Cephalanthus occidentalis*
( ) sweet pepperbush, *Clethra alnifolia*
( ) strawberry-bush, *Euonymus americanus*
( ) swamp privet, *Forestiera acuminata*
( ) witch hazel, *Hamamelis macrophylla*
( ) witch hazel, *H. virginiana*
( ) Carolina holly, *Ilex ambigua*
( ) baygall holly, *I. coriceae*
( ) possum-haw holly, *I. decidua*
( ) Georgia holly, *I. longipes*
( ) yaupon holly, *I. vomitoria*
( ) sweetspire, *Itea virginica*
( ) fetter-bush, *Leucothoe racemosa*
( ) he-huckleberry, *Lyonia ligustrina*
( ) stagger-bush, *L. mariana*
( ) Turk's cap wax-mallow, *Malvaviscus arboreus*
( ) southern wax-myrtle, *Myrica cerifera*
( ) big-leaf wax-myrtle, *M. heterophylla*
( ) acid bog wax-myrtle, *M. inodorus*
( ) low wax-myrtle, *M. pusilla*
( ) skunk-bush, *Ptelia trifoliata*
( ) red chokeberry, *Pyrus arbutifolia*
( ) Carolina buckthorn, *Rhamnus caroliniana*
( ) hoary azalea, *Rhododendron canescens*
( ) low white azalea, *R. coryi*
( ) tall white azalea, *R. oblongifolium*
( ) fragrant sumac, *Rhus aromatica*
( ) flame-leaf sumac, *R. copallina*
( ) poison sumac, *R. vernix*
( ) dwarf palmetto, *Sabal minor*
( ) elderberry, *Sambucus canadensis*
( ) Gulf sebastian-bush, *Sebastiana fruticosa*

( ) rattlebox, *Sesbania drummondii*
( ) Eve's necklace, *Sophora affinis*
( ) bristle-leaf blueberry, *Vaccinium amoenum*
( ) huckleberry, *V. arboreum*
( ) Arkansas blueberry, *V. arkansanum*
( ) Elliot's blueberry, *V. elliottii*
( ) deerberry, *V. staminium*
( ) highbush blueberry, *V. virgatum*
( ) maple-leaf viburnum, *Viburnum acerifolium*
( ) arrowwood, *V. dentatum*
( ) shiny viburnum, *V. nitidum*
( ) possum-haw viburnum, *V. nudum*
( ) plumleaf blackhaw, *V. prunifolium*
( ) blackhaw, *V. rufidulum*
( ) Louisiana yucca, *Yucca louisianensis*

Vines

( ) pepper-vine, *Ampelopsis arborea*
( ) American potato bean, *Apios americana*
( ) rattan-vine, *Berchemia scandens*
( ) cross-vine, *Bignonia capreolata*
( ) eardrop-vine, *Brunnichia ovata*
( ) cupseed, *Calycocarpum lyonii*
( ) trumpet-creeper, *Campsis radicans*
( ) butterfly pea, *Centrosema virginianum*
( ) blue jasmine, *Clematis crispa*
( ) leather-flower, *C. pitcheri*
( ) net-leaf leather flower, *C. reticulata*
( ) vase vine, *C. viornia*
( ) red-berry moonseed, *Cocculus carolinus*
( ) bindweed, *Convolvulus arvensis*
( ) dodder, *Cuscuta sp.*
( ) wild yam, *Dioscorea quarternata*
( ) Atlantic yam, *D. villosa*
( ) Carolina-jessamine, *Gelsemium sempervirens*
( ) wild potato, *Ipomea pandurata*
( ) bindweed, *I. trichocarpa*
( ) hairy clustervine, *Jacquemontia tamnifolia*
( ) Japanese honeysuckle, *Lonicera japonica*
( ) coral honeysuckle, *L. sempervirens*

( ) Japanese climbing fern, *Lygodium japonicum*
( ) pickle milkvine, *Matelia cyanchoides*
( ) milkvine, *M. decipiens*
( ) green-flowered milkvine, *M. gonocarpa*
( ) paeloncita, *Melotheria pendula*
( ) climbing hemp-weed, *Mikania scandens*
( ) Virginia creeper, *Parthenocissus quinquefolia*
( ) purple passion-flower, *Passiflora incarnata*
( ) yellow passion-flower, *P. lutea*
( ) sensitive brier, *Schrankia histricina*
( ) little-leaf sensitive brier, *S. microphylla*
( ) bull-brier, *Smilax bona-nox*
( ) saw brier, *S. glauca*
( ) bristly greenbrier, *S. hispida*
( ) laurel greenbrier, *S. laurifolia*
( ) sarsaparilla vine, *S. pumila*
( ) cat-brier, *S. rotundifolia*
( ) redbead greenbrier, *S. walterii*
( ) climbing dogbane, *Tracheolospermum difforme*
( ) summer grape, *Vitis aestivalis*
( ) sweet grape, *V. cinerea*
( ) pinewoods grape, *V. lincecumii*
( ) muscadine grape, *V. rotundifolia*
( ) wisteria, *Wisteria macrostachya*

Appendix B

Checklist, Herbaceous Plants

Note: An asterisk (*) denotes plants considered among the showiest and most popular flowers in the Big Thicket.

*( ) colic-root, *Alctris aurea*
 ( ) tooth-cup, *Ammannia coccinia*
 ( ) scarlet pimpernel, *Anagallis arrensis*
 ( ) nodding-nixie, *Apteria aphylla*
*( ) Indian-turnip or green dragon, *Arisaema dracontium*
*( ) various Dutchman's-pipes, *Arisaema* sp.
*( ) St. Andrew's cross, *Ascyrum hypericoides*
*( ) St. Peter's wort, *A. stans*
*( ) various asters, *Aster sp.*
 ( ) screw stem, *Bartonia texana*
 ( ) hairy green-eyes, *Berlandiera betonicifolia*
*( ) wine-cup, *Callirhoe papaver*
*( ) various dayflowers, *Commelina sp.*
 ( ) prairie tea, *Croton monanthogynus*
 ( ) beggars-lice, *Cynoglossum virginianum*
 ( ) finger dogshade, *Cynosciadum digitatum*
 ( ) rattlesnake-weed, *Daucus pusillus*
 ( ) various tick clovers, *Desmodium sp.*
 ( ) pony foot, *Dichondra carolinensis*
 ( ) poor Joe, *Diodia teres*
 ( ) flat-top aster, *Doellingeria umbellata*
*( ) purple coneflower, *Echinacea purpurea*
 ( ) yerba di tajo, *Elipta alba*
 ( ) elephant's-toes, *Elephantopus carolinianus*
 ( ) naked elephant's-toes, *E. nudatus*
 ( ) tobacco weed, *E. tomentosus*
 ( ) beech-drops, *Epifagus virginiana*
 ( ) various pipeworts, *Eriocaulon sp.*
*( ) yellow dog's-tooth-violet, *Erythronium rostratum*
 ( ) Joe-Pye-weed, *E. fistulosum*
 ( ) justice-weed, *E. leucolepis*
 ( ) coral bean, *Erythrina herbacea*

( ) boneset, *Eupatorium perfoliatum*
( ) wartweed, *E. helioscopia*
*( ) various gaillardia, *Gallardia sp.*
( ) various bedstraws, *Galium* sp.
*( ) white gaura, *Gaura lindheimeri*
*( ) bottle-gentian, *Gentian saponaria*
( ) various cudweeds, *Gnaphalium sp.*
*( ) various bluets, *Hadyotis sp.*
( ) low aster, *Heleastrum hemiphaericum*
*( ) Carolina rockrose, *Helianthemun carolinianum*
*( ) various asters, *Heterotheca sp.*
( ) wooly rose-mallow, *Hibiscus lasiocarpos*
*( ) rose-mallow, *H. kucophyllus*
*( ) spider-lily, *Hymenocallis liriosome*
( ) nits-and-lice, *Hypericum cistifolium*
( ) various wild lettuces, *Lactuca sp.*
( ) peppergrass, *Lepidium virginicum*
*( ) various gayfeathers, *Liatris sp.*
*( ) Carolina lily, *Lilium michauxii*
( ) toad-flax, *Linaria canadensis*
( ) clasping false pimpernel, *Lindernia anagallidea*
( ) sucker flax, *Linum medium*
( ) flax, *L. striatum*
*( ) puccoon, *Lithospermum caroliniense*
*( ) cardinal flower, *Lobelia cardinalis*
*( ) bluebonnet, *Lupinus sp.*
*( ) wild bergamont, *Monarda fistulosa*
*( ) Indian-pipe, *Monotropa uniflora*
( ) green parrot's feather, *Myriophyllum pinnatum*
*( ) purple pleat-leaf, *Nemastylis purpurea*
*( ) evening primrose, *Oenotheria heterophylla*
*( ) showy primrose, *O. speciosus*
( ) eastern prickly pear, *Opuntia compressa*
( ) tuckahoe, *Peltandra virginica*
( ) beefsteak plant, *Perilla frutescens*
( ) Christmas mistletoe, *Phoradendron serotinum*
( ) mistletoe, *P. tomentosum*
( ) stinking fleabane, *Pluchea foetida*
*( ) May-apple, *Podophyllum peltatum*
*( ) various milkworts, *Polygala sp.*

( ) great Solomon's seal, *Polygonatum commutatum*
*( ) self-heal, *Prunella vulgaris*
*( ) yellow meadow beauty, *Rhexia lutea*
*( ) Maryland meadow beauty, *R. mariana*
*( ) rose meadow beauty, *R. petiolata*

Herbaceous *( ) common meadow beauty, *R. virginica*
Plants ( ) various snoutbeans, *Rhynchosia sp.*
( ) tooth-cup, *Rotala ramosior*
( ) blackberry, *Rubus louisianus*
( ) dewberry, *R. saepescandens*
( ) curly dock, *Rumex crispus*
( ) arrowhead, *Sagittaria papillosa*
*( ) bloodroot, *Sanguinaria canadense*
*( ) lizard's-tail, *Saururus cernuus*
*( ) various skullcaps, *Scutellaria sp.*
*( ) red catchfly, *Silene subciliata*
( ) sow thistle, *Soncus asper*
*( ) Indian-pink, *Spigelia marilandica*
*( ) various noseburns, *Tragia sp.*
*( ) prairie violet, *Viola esculenta*
*( ) lance-leaved violet, *V. lanceolata*
*( ) bayou violet, *V. langloisi*
*( ) Missouri violet, *V. missouriensis*
*( ) birdfoot violet, *V. pedata*
*( ) primrose-leaved violet, *V. primulifolia*
*( ) arrow-leaf violet, *V. sagittata*
*( ) trilobed violet, *V. triloba*
*( ) Walter's violet, *V. walteri*
*( ) Texas paint brush, *Castilleja indivisa*
*( ) wild verbena, *Verbena sp.*

Checklist, Ferns, Orchids, Carnivorous Plants

Ferns

( ) ebony spleenwort, *Asplenium platyneuron*
( ) lady fern, *Athyrium felis-feminia*
( ) cut grapeleaf fern, *Botrychium disseatum*
( ) rattlesnake fern, *B. virginianum*
( ) Florida shield fern, *Dryopteris ludoviciana*
( ) southern shield fern, *D. normalis*
( ) chain fern, *Lorinsera arealata*
( ) sensitive fern, *Onoclea sensibilis*
( ) cinnamon fern, *Osmunda cinnamomea*
( ) royal fern, *O. regalis*
( ) resurrection fern, *Polypodium polypodioides*
( ) Christmas fern, *Polystichum acrostichoides*
( ) bracken fern, *Pteridium aquilinum*
( ) Florida shield fern, *Thelypteris ludoviciana*
( ) southern shield fern, *T. kunthii*
( ) Virginia chain fern, *Woodwardia virginica*

Wild Orchids

( ) bearded grass-pink, *Calopogon barbatus*
( ) grass-pink, *C. pulchellus*
( ) spring coral-root orchid, *Corallorhiza wisteriana*
( ) yellow fringed orchid, *Habaneria ciliaris*
( ) small wood orchid, *H. clavellata*
( ) ragged fringed orchid, *H. lacera*
( ) snowy orchid, *H. nivea*
( ) southern twayblade orchid, *Listera australis*
( ) rose pogonia, *Pogonia ophioglossoides*
( ) fragrant ladies' tresses orchid, *Spiranthes cernuua*
( ) green-lip ladies' tresses, *S. gracilis*
( ) grass-leaved ladies' tresses, *S. praecox*
( ) spring ladies' tresses, *S. vernalis*
( ) crippled crane-fly orchid, *Tipularia discolor*

Carnivorous Plants

( ) various sundews, *Drosera sp.*
( ) yellow pitcher-plant, *Saracenia alata*
( ) bladderworts, *Utricularia sp.*
( ) butterworts, *Pinguicula sp.*

Telephone Numbers and Addresses

Police and Emergency
911

Poison Control Center (Galveston)
(409) 765–1420

Hospitals

Beaumont
Saint Elizabeth Hospital
2830 Calder Avenue
(409) 892–7171

Baptist Hospital of Southeast
Texas
College and Eleventh Streets
(409) 835–3781

Beaumont Medical and Surgical
Hospital
3080 College Street
(409) 833–1411

Port Arthur
Saint Mary Hospital
3600 Gates Boulevard
(409) 985–7431

Jasper
Jasper Memorial Hospital
1275 Hancock
(409) 384–5461

Livingston
Livingston Memorial Hospital
602 East Church Street
(409) 327–4381

Silsbee
Silsbee Doctors Hospital
418 West Silsbee
(409) 385–5531

Woodville
Tyler County Hospital
1100 West Bluff
(409) 283–8141

Big Thicket National Preserve
Headquarters
3785 Milam
Beaumont, TX 77701
(409) 839–2689

Visitor Center
New address when completed

_____

_____

_____

New phone number _____

Ranger Station
503 Pine Street
Woodville, TX 75979
(409) 283–5824

Information Station
Kirby Nature Trailhead
(409) 246–2337

U.S. Corps of Engineers
Dam B-Town Bluff
(409) 429–3491

U.S. Forest Service
Homer Garrison Federal Bldg.
701 N. First Street
Lufkin, TX 75901
(409) 639–8501

Contacts for Possible Field Trips

Note: These groups and addresses are current as this *Guide* goes into press. Local telephone information can provide updates.

Golden Triangle Sierra Club
Judy Aronow
5590 Frost
Beaumont, TX 77706
(409) 892–9141

Houston Audubon Society
Sandi Hoover
440 Wilchester Blvd.
Houston, TX 77079
(713) 932–1932

Big Thicket Conservation Assn.
Sarah Duck
3704½ Garrott
Houston, TX 77006
(713) 524–0536

Outdoor Nature Club
Irene Leslie
5889 Valley Forge
Houston, TX 77057
(713) 796–0711

Sierra Club
Houston Regional Group
Steve Harlow
7613 Cambridge
Houston, TX
(713) 796–0711

Big Thicket Expansion Task
Force
Sierra Club
Brandt Mannchen
627 Euclid
Houston, TX 77009
(713) 861–7552

Ornithology Group
Judy Boyce
5546 Aspen
Houston, TX 77081

East Texas Herpetological
Society
Buzz Jehle
1800 Bering Drive, Suite 850
Houston, TX 77057
(713) 975–1111

Huntsville Audubon Society
Paul Culp
57 Elkins Lake
Huntsville, TX 77340
(409) 295–3404
(409) 294–1619

Dallas Sierra Club
Mike Rawlins
1512 Brentwood Dr.
Irving, TX 75601
(214) 241–9361
(214) 404–6495

Texas Committee on Natural
Resources
Morine Kovich
5934 Royal Lane, Suite 223
Dallas, TX 75230
(214) 368–1791

Other Possibilities
Biology teachers in public
schools, colleges, and
universities throughout Texas
and adjoining states take their
students on Big Thicket field
trips.

Area museums periodically
sponsor Big Thicket field
trips.

Photography classes and clubs
often arrange outings to the
Thicket, especially in spring
and fall.

For Further Reading and Reference

Note: An asterisk (*) denotes those sources useful in identifying species found in the Big Thicket.

Abernethy, Francis, ed. *Tales from the Big Thicket*. Austin: University of Texas Press, 1966.

*Ajilvsgi, Geyata. *The Wildflowers of Texas*. Fredericksburg, Tex.: Shearer Publishing, 1984.

*————. *Wild Flowers of the Big Thicket*. College Station: Texas A&M University Press, 1979.

*Brown, Clair A. *Wildflowers of Louisiana and Adjoining States*. Baton Rouge: Louisiana State University Press, 1972.

*Davis, William B. *The Mammals of Texas*. Rev. ed. Austin: Texas Parks and Wildlife Department, 1966.

Douglas, William O. *Farewell to Texas, a Vanishing Wilderness*. New York: McGraw-Hill, 1967.

Forest Trees of Texas: How to Know Them. Texas Forest Service Bulletin No. 20. College Station, 1963.

Gunter, Pete. *The Big Thicket: An Ecological Reevaluation*. Denton: University of North Texas Press, 1993.

Hamric, Roy, ed. *Archer Fullingim: A Country Editor's View of Life*. Austin: Heidelberg Publishers, 1975.

Johnston, Maxine. *Thicket Explorer*. Saratoga, Tex.: Museum Publication Series No. 3, 1973.

Lasswell, Mary. *I'll Take Texas*. Boston: Houghton Mifflin, 1958.

McLeod, Claude. *The Big Thicket of East Texas*. Huntsville: Sam Houston Press, 1967.

Metzler, Susan, and Van Metzler. *Texas Mushrooms*. Austin: University of Texas Press, 1992.

Parks, H. B.; V. L. Cory; and others. *Survey of the East Texas Big Thicket Area*. 1938. 2nd edition, Saratoga, Tex.: Big Thicket Association, 1971.

Peacock, Howard. *The Big Thicket of Texas: America's Ecological Wonder*. Boston: Little, Brown and Co., 1984.

———, ed. *The Nature of Texas*. College Station: Texas A&M University Press, 1991

*Peterson, Roger Tory. *A Field Guide to the Birds of Eastern and Central North America*. Boston: Houghton Mifflin, 1980.

*Vines, Robert A. *Trees of East Texas*. Austin: University of Texas Press, 1977.

*———. *Trees, Shrubs and Woody Vines of the Southwest*. Austin: University of Texas Press, 1960.

Watson, Geraldine. *Big Thicket Plant Ecology*. Saratoga, Tex.: Museum Publication Series No. 5, 1975.

Further Reading

Index

Index

Index

Nature Lover's Guide to the Big Thicket was composed into type using Magna software and output on an Agfa Selectset 5000 in ten point Menion with two points of spacing between the lines. Menion was also selected for display. The book was designed by Cameron Poulter, typeset by Connell-Zeko Type and Graphics, printed offset by Hart Graphics, Inc., and bound by Custom Bookbindery. The paper on which this book is printed carries acid-free characteristics for an effective life of at least three hundred years.

TEXAS A&M UNIVERSITY PRESS : COLLEGE STATION